Cambridge Elements ≡

Elements in Public Policy
edited by
M. Ramesh
National University of Singapore (NUS)
Michael Howlett
Simon Fraser University, British Colombia
Xun Wu
Hong Kong University of Science and Technology
Judith Clifton
University of Cantabria
Eduardo Araral
National University of Singapore (NUS)

DIGITAL TECHNOLOGY, POLITICS, AND POLICY-MAKING

Fabrizio Gilardi
University of Zurich

CAMBRIDGE
UNIVERSITY PRESS

CAMBRIDGE
UNIVERSITY PRESS

University Printing House, Cambridge CB2 8BS, United Kingdom

One Liberty Plaza, 20th Floor, New York, NY 10006, USA

477 Williamstown Road, Port Melbourne, VIC 3207, Australia

314–321, 3rd Floor, Plot 3, Splendor Forum, Jasola District Centre,
New Delhi – 110025, India

103 Penang Road, #05–06/07, Visioncrest Commercial, Singapore 238467

Cambridge University Press is part of the University of Cambridge.

It furthers the University's mission by disseminating knowledge in the pursuit of
education, learning, and research at the highest international levels of excellence.

www.cambridge.org
Information on this title: www.cambridge.org/9781108744904
DOI: 10.1017/9781108887304

Fabrizio Gilardi 2022

First published 2022

A catalogue record for this publication is available from the British Library.

ISBN 978-1-108-74490-4 Paperback
ISSN 2398-4058 (online)
ISSN 2514-3565 (print)

Digital Technology, Politics, and Policy-Making

Elements in Public Policy

DOI: 10.1017/9781108887304
First published online: May 2022

Fabrizio Gilardi
University of Zurich
Author for correspondence: Fabrizio Gilardi, gilardi@ipz.uzh.ch

Abstract: This Element shows, based on a review of the literature, how digital technology has affected liberal democracies, with a focus on three key aspects of democratic politics: political communication, political participation, and policy-making. The impact of digital technology permeates the entire political process, affecting the flow of information among citizen and political actors, the connection between the mass public and political elites, and the development of policy responses to societal problems. This Element discusses how digital technology has shaped these different domains, identifies areas of research consensus as well as unresolved questions, and argues that a key perspective involves issue definition, that is, how the nature of the problems raised by digital technology is subject to political contestation.

Keywords: social media, fake news, civic tech, e-government, artificial intelligence, algorithms

ISBNs: 9781108744904 (PB), 9781108887304 (OC)
ISSNs: 2398-4058 (online), 2514-3565 (print)

Contents

1 The Digital Transformation of Politics and Policy-Making

1.1 Introduction

The rise of digital technology has been the best of times and also the worst, a roller-coaster of hopes and fears: "social media have gone – in the popular imagination at least – from being a way for pro-democratic forces to fight autocrats to being a tool of outside actors who want to attack democracies" (Tucker et al., 2017, 47). The 2016 US presidential election raised fundamental questions regarding the compatibility of the Internet with democracy (Persily, 2017). The divergent assessments of the promises and risks of digital technology have to do, in part, with the fact that it has become such a pervasive phenomenon. Whether digital technology is, on balance, a net benefit or harm for democratic processes and institutions depends on which specific aspects we focus on. Moreover, the assessment is not value neutral, because digital technology has become inextricably linked with our politics. As Farrell (2012, 47) argued a few years ago, "[a]s the Internet becomes politically normalized, it will be ever less appropriate to study it in isolation but ever more important to think clearly, and carefully, about its relationship to politics." Reflecting on this issue requires going beyond the headlines, which tend to focus on the most dramatic concerns and may have a negativity bias common in news reporting in general. The shortage of hard facts in this area, linked to the singular challenges of studying the connection between digital technology and politics, exacerbates the problem.

Since it affects virtually every aspect of politics and policy-making, the nature and effects of digital technology have been studied from many different angles in increasingly fragmented literatures. For example, studies of disinformation and social media usually do not acknowledge research on the usage of artificial intelligence (AI) in public administration – for good reasons, because such is the nature of specialized academic research. Similarly, media attention tends to concentrate on the most newsworthy aspects, such as the role of Facebook in elections, without connecting them to other related phenomena. The compartmentalization of academic and public attention in this area is understandable, but it obscures the relationships that exist among the different parts. Moreover, the fact that scholarly and media attention are sometimes out of sync might lead policy-makers to focus on solutions before there is a scientific consensus on the nature and scale of the problems. For example, policy-makers may emphasize curbing "fake news" while there is still no agreement in the research community about its effects on political outcomes.

This Element shows, based on a review of the literature, how digital technology has affected liberal democracies across the political process, with a

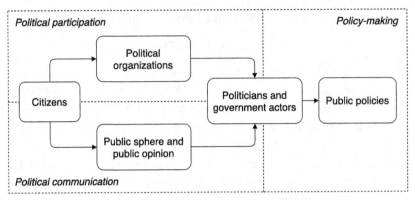

Figure 1 Stylized model of democratic politics (adapted from Fung et al., 2013, 32)

focus on three key aspects: political communication, political participation, and policy-making. Political communication "refers to the flow of information and the exchange of messages among political actors, citizens, and the media" (Esser and Pfetsch, 2020, 336); political participation "establishes links from the mass public to the political elites" (Kitschelt and Rehm, 2020, 318); and policy-making involves "the elaboration and discussion of policy solutions to societal problems" (Knill and Tosun, 2020, 361). These three areas are linked to the key elements of democratic politics, as shown in stylized form in Figure 1. Taken together, they cover many key elements such as elections and referendums, political behavior, collective action, political communication, decision-making, and government and public administration.

Using the model displayed in Figure 1, Fung et al. (2013) elaborated several scenarios regarding the possible effects of digital technology on democratic politics, each focusing on a specific element of the democratic process. The first scenario considered political communication, and posited that digital technology might strengthen the public sphere. The second scenario focused on policy-making, and hypothesized that digital technology might enable citizens to have a direct effect on public action, effectively by-passing established institutional channels. The third scenario, anchored in the area of political participation, recognized the potential of digital technology to enhance direct democracy and establish a more direct link between citizens and policy-makers. The fourth scenario, called "truth-based advocacy," cuts across political participation and communication by arguing that digital technology may empower advocacy groups to shape the public sphere by advancing "new and important truths" (Fung et al., 2013, 38) – or, we could say, their own framing of facts and problems. Fifth, again in the area of political participation, the constituent-mobilization scenario highlighted the new possibilities for political

Figure 2 The digital transformation of politics and policy-making in the news.

organizations to engage their members and conduct campaigns using digital technology. Finally, the sixth scenario recognized how digital technology may make it possible for decision-makers to crowdsource the identification of problems as well as the development of potential solutions. The purpose of this Element is not to evaluate the empirical merits of these six scenarios. Instead, I rely on Fung et al. (2013) to identify three key areas for the political impact of digital technology (political participation, political communication, and policy-making) as well as their connections, which are discussed most explicitly in Section 5.

The diversity and scope of the digital transformation of politics and policy-making is illustrated by the headlines in Figure 2. The examples include algorithmic decision-making, facial recognition and privacy, the regulation of AI, political ads on Facebook, antitrust and tech platforms, political participation ("clicktivism"), and election disinformation on YouTube. At first sight, these headlines might not necessarily have a lot in common. In the public perception, the influence of social media on elections does not share much with the regulation of AI, nor with monopoly policy. Similarly, academic research is necessarily specialized and studies specific problems in relatively narrow areas. But the examples in Figure 2 are part of the same overarching reality: the power of digital technology to change how political decisions are made. With reference to Figure 1, disinformation and online political ads are linked to political communication; "clicktivism" touches on new forms of online participation;

and mentions of AI show how policy-making processes integrate new technologies while at the same time attempting to regulate them. Taken together, these different aspects of digital technology pervade the whole process of democratic politics.

The examples in Figure 2 also illustrate another feature. Many agree that digital technology is causing political problems, but there is no agreement regarding the nature of those problems – nor, consequently, what adequate policy responses to those problems might be. The headline "Congress agrees big tech creepy, can't agree how" is tongue in cheek, but it illustrates the point very well. One reason for the lack of consensus is that establishing basic facts in this area is very hard. Much of the data needed to give clear answers to questions such as "who spreads disinformation on social media?" or "how do algorithms discriminate against some groups?" belongs to tech companies, which have shown little inclination to share this data with academic researchers, civil society groups, journalists, or even governments. Lack of transparency means that researchers working independent of the tech platforms cannot generate accurate knowledge, much less make steps toward a scientific consensus. Of course, agreement among experts is no guarantee for political consensus, as we know all too well from the cases of climate change and the COVID-19 pandemic. However, the shortage of established facts makes it even more difficult for policy-makers to agree on an effective course of action.

While the fragility of empirical findings is real, the fact that policy-makers cannot easily agree on the nature of problems, much less on policy responses, is not specific to digital technology and politics. Instead, it is a defining feature of any political process. No issue inherently requires political solutions: "social conditions do not automatically generate policy actions" (Baumgartner and Jones, 1993, 27). Instead, political actors construct arguments regarding the nature of a given problem and link them to the solutions (policies) they favor to address it. Some see the use of facial recognition technology by government authorities as a dangerous state surveillance tool, while others emphasize benefits such as finding missing children or catching terrorists; some see digital media as a major threat to democracies and suggest breaking up "big tech," while others argue that regulations would stifle their innovation capacities, upon which much of the economy relies. The 2018 hearings of Facebook's CEO Mark Zuckerberg in the US Congress and the EU Parliament revealed how politicians are trying to make sense of the potential dangers that digital technology presents to our democracies, and what kind political response, if any, is appropriate. As one commentator put it: "If lawmakers want to regulate Facebook, they might need to get on the same page about what problem they're trying to solve."[1] While many share the view that digital technology has caused significant problems that politics should address, there is no consensus on what those problems actually are. As elaborated in Section 5, the issue-definition stage – a key part of any policy-making process – is particularly salient in the case of digital technology and politics.

1.2 Researching the Digital Transformation of Politics and Policy-Making

From a social science perspective, a distinctive feature of research on digital technology and politics is that it is like a sandcastle: it is hard to do and quick to decay. To some extent, this statement is true for much of social science research, but the specific combination of research challenges and decay of findings is particularly striking for digital technology and politics.

First, a unique feature of research on digital technology and politics is that answering many questions, such as the prevalence of misinformation or the role of algorithms for decision-making, or the spread of political information, not only requires access to data that belong to platforms, but also that access is almost entirely up to the goodwill of platforms themselves. This state of affairs has been described as "post-API age" (Freelon, 2018) and "APIcalypse" (Bruns, 2019), with reference to the decision of many platforms, Facebook in particular, to limit data access by closing Application Programming Interfaces (APIs) or severely limiting their functionalities, which previously permitted relatively wide searchable access to their content. The decisions were linked to a tension between data access and the protection of personal data that escalated in the context of the Cambridge Analytica scandal, in which researchers abused Facebook's terms of service to sell psychometric analyses that the media portrayed as contributing to Donald Trump's election in 2016. Although the data leak likely played no role in the election, it increased the salience of data protection in the media and on political agendas. The pushback prompted Facebook and other platforms to lock down their data and, thereby, to throw out the baby with the bathwater. Since then, researchers and policy-makers have struggled to come up with arrangements that would require platforms to supply the data needed to answer important questions (such as the actual role of Cambridge Analytica in the 2016 election) while ensuring data protection. The European Union's General Data Protection Regulation (GDPR) includes a research exception to its strict data protection rules, but its scope and application are unclear. As recently as 2020, the European Data Protection Supervisor

---

[1] www.vox.com/policy-and-politics/2018/4/10/17222062/mark-zuckerberg-testimony-graham-facebook-regulations.

concluded that "the full extent of this special regime is not precisely delineated" (European Data Protection Supervisor, 2020, 18).

The research community has recognized these challenges and attempted to overcome them in various ways (Persily and Tucker, 2020a). One of the most ambitious initiatives was Social Science One, a high-profile project led by Harvard and Stanford researchers aiming to provide an institutional interface between the scholarly community and Facebook, to square the circle of ensuring both data access and protection (King and Persily, 2020). It is revealing of the challenges the research community faces that Social Science One had to reduce its ambitions significantly despite the major, public commitment of some of the most influential academic actors in this space. Other large-scale institutional efforts currently underway include the European Digital Media Observatory (EDMO), supported by the European Union.[2] At a smaller scale, several groups of researchers have recognized the need to construct research infrastructures with pipelines combining data collection, processing, and analysis (Lazer et al., 2020; Gilardi et al., 2022a; Watts et al., 2021). Such infrastructures do not solve the problem of data access per se, but they help address "the need to develop and maintain the skills that are required to observe platforms" (Rieder and Hofmann, 2020, 23). Moreover, they facilitate collaborative research through a division of labor between data collection and analysis. A further benefit of these kinds of infrastructures is that they help researchers respond quickly to developments such as the new Twitter API for Academic Research launched in 2021, and a similar API Facebook is planning to release. Some of these details will probably be outdated by the time they reach readers of this Element, but the bottom line is likely to hold. Data access is difficult for researchers and subject to conditions set primarily by platforms, which may change quickly and risk derailing planned or ongoing projects.

The second distinctive challenge of research on digital technology and politics is that it is particularly vulnerable to "knowledge decay" (Munger, 2019). The external validity of findings is fragile, to a higher degree than is the case in other areas. There are two dimensions to this problem: time and space. On the one hand, scholars have to deal with "internet time" (Karpf, 2012). The nature of digital environments is extremely dynamic and changing. Platforms constantly tweak their features and algorithms in ways that remain hidden to outsiders. Moreover, the user base of platforms also changes, sometimes quite quickly. The context in which a given study is conducted never remains constant, nor even relatively stable. Consequently, we must face the sad but true fact that "research findings are rendered obsolete by the time they have been

---

[2] https://edmo.eu/.

published" (Karpf, 2012, 642). The slow publication process typical of social science journals does not help. Moreover, knowledge decay is transmitted not only over time but across space. Although things are improving, a significant chunk of knowledge on digital technology and politics is based on research done on the US case. While most researchers are aware that "[a]ny uncritical generalizations on the role of digital media in politics based on cases and findings from the United States is obviously deeply naive" (Jungherr et al., 2020, 7), sometimes the best or even only empirical evidence available is based on the United States, in no small part due to the data access issues discussed earlier in this section. On top of the US focus of much research are some blind spots of that literature, for example, regarding race and ethnicity (Kreiss, 2021). Although most social science struggles with generalization, the temporal and spatial restrictions typical of much research on digital technology and politics limit the empirical basis of many claims, including those aiming to establish basic descriptive facts (Munger et al., 2021).

For these reasons, researchers have sometimes struggled to determine what we talk about when we talk about digital technology and politics. The problem also concerns politics and policy-making. Actors making political decisions face unusual challenges in the area of digital technology (Taeihagh et al., 2021). In part, this is due to research gaps, which force policy-makers to come up with solutions for problems that are not well understood. As Persily (2021, 2) put it, "[t]he U.S. government, like its counterparts around the world, is rushing headstrong and blind toward regulation without a complete understanding of the problems they wish to solve." With qualifications, the statement applies to most areas discussed in this Element.

1.3 Scope of the Element

There is an enormous amount of work on digital technology and politics, fragmented into multiple separate literatures. A comprehensive review is impossible. This Element concentrates on liberal democracies and, therefore, does not consider explicitly consequential questions such as censorship (e.g., King et al., 2013; Roberts, 2018; Pan and Siegel, 2020), human rights (e.g., Dragu and Lupu, 2021), interstate or intrastate conflicts (e.g., Zeitzoff, 2017), state repression (e.g., Weidmann and Rød, 2019; Gohdes, 2020), and cybersecurity (e.g., Branch, 2020). These are obviously very important topics, but they are outside of the scope of this Element. Moreover, I acknowledge that the focus is squarely on social science research. Philosophy, ethics, and law inform many of the works discussed in this Element, but they are not the primary focus. Within this scope, the Element takes stock of the available knowledge through a comprehensive (though, unavoidably, not exhaustive) review of several literatures that are quite distinct, and shows how they fit together using the model of democratic politics shown in Figure 1. By contrast, other works are focused squarely on specific aspects of digital technology and politics, such as social media (e.g., Settle, 2018; Woolley and Howard, 2018; Aral, 2020; Persily and Tucker, 2020b). Jungherr et al. (2020) is one of the most comprehensive books on the subject, arguing that digital media have not transformed politics fundamentally, but have "retooled" it. In this perspective, the core needs of political actors, such as accessing and creating political information or coordinating with others, have remained the same. Instead of changing these needs, digital media affect how political actors and organizations address them, notably by facilitating the flow of information as well as the connections among actors in networks. In contrast to Jungherr et al. (2020), this Element is less focused on digital technology as a communication tool. While political communication is discussed in depth in Section 2, the Element also considers explicitly the role of digital technology for two other key elements of democratic politics: political participation (Section 3) and policy-making (Section 4). Building on the insights of the previous sections, Section 5 makes the case that considering the link between "problems" and "solutions," and specifically the ways in which the connection is politically contested, is an important angle from which to understand the digital transformation of politics and policy-making.

1.4 Preview

Section 2 focuses on how digital technology has reshaped the flow of political information. In the aftermath of Donald Trump's election in 2016, the perception that social media spread misinformation and increased political polarization has been widely shared. The popularity of some COVID-19 conspiracy theories on social media has reinforced this impression. It is now commonplace to argue that platforms like Facebook, YouTube, and Twitter can sway elections and cause a range of undesirable outcomes. Online political ads that can be targeted to specific groups are perceived to enable the creation of echo chambers and filter bubbles in which discording opinions are excluded. Twitter has given a megaphone to fringe views and a channel to influence mainstream media. And YouTube's reliance on recommendation algorithms is thought to push users down rabbit holes of conspiracy and extremism. Importantly, researching these platforms is hard, such that identifying key facts is harder than it may seem. Section 2 discusses key research findings in this and other areas related to political communication, including the prevalence and effects of fake news, echo chambers and filter bubbles, and online political advertising.

Section 3 turns to the connection between digital technology and political participation. In most countries, the principal channel through which citizens participate in politics is elections, which mostly require paper ballots. Given the ubiquity of internet banking and shopping, internet voting may seem a logical extension that should have been implemented long ago. Indeed, several countries have experimented with internet voting, but significant tail risks regarding the security of elections, coupled with mixed evidence regarding benefits for political participation, have prevented its widespread adoption. Another way in which digital tools have been embedded in elections is Voting Advice Applications (VAAs), which match voters with candidates and parties based on surveys of policy preferences. Elections, however, take place infrequently and are restricted to a relatively small subset of the population (those with voting rights). Digital technology has been a key component of activism, both online and offline, which can benefit marginalized groups disadvantaged by existing power structures. Moreover, digital technology has blurred the line between different forms of collective actions, as movements that emerged in digital spaces may institutionalize as political parties.

Section 4 considers how digital technology has affected policy-making across the policy cycle. In a first step, issues have to be perceived as politically salient, and social media has played an increasingly important role in such agenda-setting processes. In the policy formulation stage, digital tools make it possible to include a broader range of groups and individuals, on the one hand with a focus on the generation of new ideas with the inputs of large numbers of people, and on the other with a more explicit emphasis on the value of participation as such. In both the policy formulation and implementation stages, an important trend has been the increased reliance on data and algorithms to make and enforce decisions. In combination, data and algorithms promise to improve the efficiency and effectiveness of policies, but tools such as facial recognition and other uses of AI raise important issues related to data protection, privacy, as well as ethical and legal questions. For example, how is the usage of AI to assist decision-making compatible with the right to due process, and can it avoid the reproduction of existing biases? Many of the problems are linked to the opacity of algorithms, whose functioning often cannot be fully understood even by experts, much less users within public administration or the general public.

Section 5 elaborates on the themes developed in the previous sections in two ways. First, it discusses the areas in which a certain degree of consensus can be

identified in the literature, as well as the questions that remain unanswered or
are most actively debated from a social science perspective. Political communication is the domain most affected by the research challenges described in Section 1.2. Therefore, while there is increasing agreement that the most extreme
claims regarding the reach and consequences of misinformation are probably
exaggerated, a thorough assessment of the implications of social media for
political communication (and democracy more broadly) has remained elusive,
since it would require a much greater degree of transparency from tech companies that, realistically, could only be achieved through government regulation.
By contrast, knowledge in the area of political participation stands on much
firmer ground, particularly regarding voting, whereas research on activist forms
of participation is one of the most dynamic and interesting from a social science perspective. Regarding policy-making, the field is quite diverse and lacks
integration. Several topics, such as crowdsourcing and civic tech, would benefit
from stronger engagement from social scientists, whereas algorithmic decision-
making is an important area in which social science research has made valuable
contributions (for example, to assess biases and accountability problems) and
which remains very dynamic. Second, Section 1.2 elaborates on the relevance
of problem definition as a theoretical angle to address most of the themes discussed in the Element across the whole political process. The relatively new,
highly technical nature of the issues, coupled with the opacity of tech platforms,
implies that the nature of the problems raised by digital technology, and therefore of the policy responses advanced to address them, are highly contested.
Moreover, political contestation is shaped by digital technology itself, through
the mechanisms discussed in the Element. The section illustrates the argument
with two cases – the regulation content moderation and artificial intelligence –
and concludes with the proposition that problem definition is a key perspective
from which to understand how politics responds to digital technology.

2 Political Communication

Political communication refers to the process by which information is created
and disseminated among political actors (Esser and Pfetsch, 2020, 337). This
process is a key component of democratic politics in that it reflects "the ability of contributors to political communication spaces to introduce, amplify,
and maintain topics, frames, and speakers that come to dominate political discourse" (Jungherr et al., 2019, 3). These processes can be systematized using
the notion of the political communication ecosystem, which includes traditional media, social media, and channels controlled directly by political actors
and connects them with the citizens and the general public (Esser and Pfetsch,

2020, 340). Digital technology has affected this ecosystem by changing the relative power of different actors, accelerating the fragmentation of the media system and public sphere, and facilitating the spread of misleading information (Esser and Pfetsch, 2020, 338). Against this background, this section focuses on three major areas in which digital technology has affected political communication: first, disinformation, misinformation, and related phenomena commonly discussed under the label "fake news"; second, the fragmentation of the public sphere and its potential for increasing political polarization; and third, new options available to political actors to influence public opinion via online advertising.

2.1 Fake News

A key element of digitized political communication ecosystems is that information of any kind can spread very quickly, including information that is deceptive and potentially harmful. This phenomenon is often referred to as "fake news," which can be defined as "false or misleading messages spread under the guise of informative content, whether in the form of elite communication, online messages, advertising, or published articles" (Guess and Lyons, 2020, 10). There are three important elements in this definition: first, the *content* of the message is false or at least misleading; second, the *form* of the message is deceptive, in that it is made to look like conventional information even though it is not; and third, the *medium* is irrelevant, that is, messages can be disseminated over any channel (not just online) and in any format (text, images, video). A relevant distinction is that between disinformation and misinformation, which bears on the intentionality of the harm that is potentially caused, as shown in Table 1. From this perspective, disinformation is defined as "all forms of false, inaccurate, or misleading information designed, presented and promoted to intentionally cause public harm or for profit" (European Commission, 2018, 11). Misinformation, on the other hand, implies no intention to harm, regardless of whether the messages are actually harmful or not. Although useful analytically, the distinction is admittedly hard to make in practice since the intention to deceive cannot be easily determined (Nyhan, 2020, 220–221). The bottom row in Table 1 shows that some messages may be harmful even though they are not deceptive according to the definition above – that is, the messages are not disguised as informative. In that case, scholars speak of "malinformation," which includes intentionally harmful behaviors such as hate speech, harassment, and leaks (Wardle and Derakhshan, 2017).

Research on fake news has addressed several questions, which could be answered with different degrees of reliability, due to the challenges discussed in Section 1.2. They include the prevalence of fake news and engagement with

Table 1 Unpacking "fake news"

| | | Intentionally harmful | |
		Yes	No
Deceptive	Yes	Disinformation	Misinformation
	No	Malinformation	Information

it, its effects on political outcomes such as voting behavior, the role of different actors in generating and spreading it, and the kinds of interventions that may help mitigate it.

The prevalence and reach of disinformation has been a contentious issue. In the aftermath of the 2016 US presidential elections, journalistic accounts suggested that disinformation is widespread on social media, and a large-scale study demonstrated that on Twitter, false news, especially that with political content, spread to a much greater extent than other news (Vosoughi et al., 2018). However, research later provided evidence that questioned some of these early assessments. Allcott and Gentzkow (2017) relied on survey experiments to estimate the percentage of the US population that was exposed to fake news, concluding that, on average, US voters saw just over one "fake news" item during the 2016 election campaign. Other studies, using different methods and data that usually identify fake news based on its source, confirmed that fake news is not a mass phenomenon, in the sense that most people neither see nor spread it. Instead, consumption and dissemination is concentrated in a small group of people who are older, more conservative, and more interested in politics than the general population (Grinberg et al. 2019; Guess, Lyons et al. 2019; Guess, Nagler, and Tucker 2019; Allen et al. 2020; Guess, Nyhan, and Reifler 2020). The fact that older people seem more vulnerable to fake news can be explained in different ways: cognitive decline leading to remembering the information but not the source; social changes such as increased trust in older age and greater difficulty in detecting lies; and digital illiteracy, namely less familiarity with digital tools (Brashier and Schacter, 2020). Other studies focused on the cognitive mechanisms underlying susceptibility to fake news more in general; for example, contrasting "motivated reasoning" (the idea that belief in fake news is driven by their alignment with political beliefs) with "classical reasoning" (the capacity to think analytically) (Pennycook and Rand, 2019b). Focusing on sharing behavior, and specifically the fact that most people do not engage with fake news, experimental findings suggest that reputation is an important factor: fake news hurts the reputation of those who share it even when it is in line with the political beliefs of those it is shared with (Altay et al., 2020). Another line of work concentrates not on the people believing fake news, but on its content and sources. Some studies found that the novelty of fake news is a significant factor for its spread (Vosoughi et al., 2018; Altay et al., 2020). People are more likely to share accurate than fake news, but "interestingness" can compensate for some lack of accuracy (Altay et al., 2020). Furthermore, sources matter: an experiment found that users are more likely to believe fake news if it comes from sources that previously supplied them with information congruent with their political beliefs (Bauer and von Hohenberg, 2020).

Can fake news change the outcomes of elections? Answering this question directly is extremely difficult because elections are real-world events that cannot be manipulated by researchers in ways that would allow measuring the aggregate effects of fake news. Therefore, available evidence is more indirect and relies on the persuasive effects of fake news at the individual level, often measured using survey experiments (e.g., Loomba et al., 2021), which cannot be easily extrapolated to the level of whole elections. One study found a positive but imprecise relationship between exposure to fake news and changes in vote intention and turnout, which can only rule out large effects in the order of ten percentage points (Guess et al., 2020). How such inconsistent effects would translate in aggregate outcomes is hard to determine, but it is conceivable that they may play a significant role in close elections. Another study, focusing on coordinated disinformation efforts, also failed to find effects on public opinion (Bail et al., 2020). Twitter users who interacted with troll accounts operated by the Internet Research Agency experienced no change in political attitudes and behaviors, possibly because most interactions occurred among users who already held strong opinions, which tend to be stable. The fact that Russian bots found more resonance in this group of users is indicative that disinformation phenomena do not affect the broader population, as other studies have also found, and suggests that the direct effects of disinformation are likely quite small. However, even though disinformation does not necessarily change election outcomes, it may affect democratic processes in other ways. From a deliberative perspective, which emphasizes the importance of citizens coming together to discuss problems and solutions, online disinformation poses three challenges (McKay and Tenove, 2020). It promotes "epistemic cynicism," that is, the belief that there is no point trying to agree on facts; it increases "affective polarization," namely the dislike of others holding different views; and it derails good-faith discussions by increasing suspicions about the motives or even identities of participants in discussions. These features are specific to, or at least intensified in, online environments.

The effects of disinformation may be linked to its form. For example, "deepfakes" are highly realistic videos created or manipulated using AI technology to represent politicians or public figures in deceptive ways. Arguably, they could have a bigger impact than more rudimentary forms of disinformation. However, early findings suggest that although deepfakes may not be that different from conventional fake news when it comes to their direct persuasive effects, they may induce a broader skepticism toward news in general. Regarding direct effect, findings are mixed: there is evidence that political deepfakes do not mislead viewers (Vaccari and Chadwick, 2020); that they do mislead viewers, although not more than traditional fake news in textual or audio format (Barari et al., 2021); and that people are unable to discriminate between real and fake videos (Ternovski et al., 2021). These findings should be put in the context of research on the persuasive effects of video in general, which have been found to be minimal (Wittenberg et al., 2020). Importantly, both Vaccari and Chadwick (2020) and Ternovski et al. (2021) point to the indirect negative consequences of deepfakes, which may contribute to "a climate of indeterminacy about truth and falsity that, in turn, diminishes trust in online news" (Vaccari and Chadwick, 2020, 2).

An interesting question is whether the perceived dangers of fake news might not be more harmful than its actual effects (Jungherr and Schroeder, 2021). The discussion of "fake news" by traditional media has been characterized as a "moral panic," namely "public anxiety that a particular social threat will lead to declining standards" (Carlson, 2020, 375). In the case of fake news, "the journalistic community has created a deviant other in fake news while supporting its own accounts as truthful and trustworthy" (Carlson, 2020, 375). The discourse surrounding fake news, and the usage of the term by different actors, is an interesting question that certainly deserves more attention (Egelhofer and Lecheler, 2019), and which is linked to the issue definition processes discussed in Section 5.2.

An important insight is that, despite the significance of online spaces, traditional media play a significant role in the spread of disinformation (Karpf, 2020). The media ecosystem – the ways in which different media are linked together – is fundamentally asymmetric in that it is self-contained on the right but more interconnected on the left (Benkler et al., 2018; Benkler, 2020). This feature is only loosely related to the Internet and social media, but is crucial to understand the spread of disinformation. When fake news items trend online, they can reach mainstream media, which expand their reach beyond online audiences via the interconnection of social and traditional media that characterizes hybrid media systems. Moreover, beyond amplifying fake news that is already circulating online, political and media elites can be a direct driver: "political misinformation often originates at the elite level from sources such as politicians, pundits, and ideological or partisan groups and media outlets" (Nyhan, 2020, 227). This fact is sometimes referred to with the shorthand "disinformation comes from the top." Although the phenomenon is widely recognized, it remains understudied (Weeks and Gil de Zúñiga, 2021, 282). In addition to their role in amplifying, generating, and spreading fake news, another way in which elites matter is through their discourse, that is, the ways in which they talk about fake news as a problem (Egelhofer and Lecheler, 2019). For example, results from a survey experiment suggest that exposure to statements on fake news by political elites reduces the accuracy with which people identify real news as well as trust in media (Van Duyn and Collier, 2019).

What can be done to counter fake news? Table 2 compares several strategies based on the target and the timing of the interventions. Targets include individuals (potentially) exposed to fake news, political elites (which, as discussed previously, are important actors in the spread of fake news), and online platforms as the channels through which fake news spread. Starting with individuals, digital literacy efforts may give people the tools to screen out fake news and therefore prevent consumption in the first place. Simple interventions aiming to help people distinguish between real and fake news, such as enhancing skepticism toward implausible headlines, may reduce the perceived accuracy of false as well as real news (Guess et al., 2020). However, the effect is larger for false news, such that the overall gap between beliefs in real and false news is increased. The effects may also vary across subsamples, meaning that different groups may react in different ways to digital literacy interventions.

Once individuals have been exposed to fake news, the task is to correct any misperceptions that may ensue. Unfortunately, this task is not straightforward (Lazer et al., 2018). Efforts to correct misinformation may be insufficient and even counterproductive (Wittenberg and Berinski, 2020). First, corrections may reduce but not erase misperceptions; second, they may backfire and even strengthen the false beliefs. For example, experiments found that the effects of corrections are conditional on the ideology of respondents, and may even be negative – they may backfire – among some ideological subgroups (Nyhan and Reifler, 2010). These findings, however, were later themselves corrected, so to speak, in a set of large experiments covering many different issues (Wood and Porter, 2019). This replication failed to find support for backfire effects, and concluded that individuals usually update their perceptions based on new factual information presented to them, even when the evidence goes against their ideology. A further study conducted during the 2016 US presidential campaign confirmed this result, finding that fact-checks improve the accuracy of factual beliefs across the ideological spectrum (Nyhan et al., 2020).

Table 2 Strategies for countering fake news (adapted from Nyhan, 2020, 230).

	Beforehand	Afterwards
Individuals	Digital literacy	Corrections
Online platforms	Block untrustworthy sources	Fact-checking, reducing reach
Political elites	Reputational incentives	Reputational sanctions

Turning to online platforms, one way to prevent fake news from spreading is by blocking untrustworthy sources. However, such a strategy raises important questions regarding free speech. Platforms can also attempt to counter fake news ex post, once content has been allowed (implicitly or explicitly) to be published. Fact-checking is an intervention by which content is labeled as "true" or "false," or "disputed." A key issue is how such labels are produced, and by whom. Although professional fact-checking organizations exist, they may have insufficient capacity to tackle the scale of the problem while ensuring a balanced approach across the political spectrum. Crowdsourcing has been suggested as an alternative way to identify trustworthy sources. Research shows that laypeople across the political spectrum are able to produce reliable ratings, which could be used by algorithms to down-rank content from sources that the crowd considers dubious (Pennycook and Rand, 2019a). Even if reliable fact-checking labels can be produced at scale, the question remains how effective they are. That might depend on how the labels are presented to users. Specifically, both "Rated false" and "Disputed" tags reduce belief in false information, more so than a general warning to beware of misleading content, but "Rated false" is more effective than "Disputed" (Clayton et al., 2020). Importantly, general warnings may decrease belief in the accuracy of true as well as of false news. Therefore, Freeze et al. (2020) warns that "general warnings of misinformation should be avoided as indiscriminate use can reduce the credibility of valid news sources and lead individuals to discard useful information." Another issue is *when* fact-checking labels should be shown to users. An experiment found that such labels are most effective in the long term (after a week) if the labels are displayed after users read content ("debunking") than during ("labeling") or before ("prebunking") reading it (Brashier et al., 2021).

Finally, the bottom row of Table 2 recognizes that political elites play an important role. Interventions at this level are the most problematic. Reputational incentives have been shown to have some effectiveness in restraining the sharing behavior of regular users (Altay et al., 2020), and a similar effect might also apply to elites. Consistent with this view is the finding that legislators who were randomly alerted to the reputational risks of spreading dubious information were subsequently less likely to receive poor ratings by fact-checkers (Nyhan and Reifler, 2015). On the other hand, the wider incentive structures of political elites, including the interaction between social and traditional media in "hybrid media systems" (Chadwick, 2017), as well as the role of echo chambers and political polarization, suggest that the reputational incentives of political elites are currently not well aligned with reigning in the spread of fake news. Reputational sanctions for elite actors who engage in disinformation is the last strategy in Table 2. To what extent political elites pay reputational costs for misbehavior is an open question. The arguments just discussed suggest that the costs, at least those imposed by voters, may be limited. A more extreme form of sanction is blocking access to social media platforms ("deplatforming"), which is a problematic approach because it raises thorny questions regarding free speech, particularly in the United States. We will return to this question in Section 5.2.

2.2 Echo Chambers and Filter Bubbles

The notion of "echo chambers" refers to a potential feature of online spaces that was recognized twenty years ago and has captivated public debates ever since (Sunstein, 2001, 2018). The idea is that the abundance of choices available online make it possible for people to create their own information niche in which their views are reinforced while excluding other ideas, thus undermining a common frame of reference or shared experiences. The argument is based on the notion of "selective exposure," which posits that "people prefer exposure to communications that agree with their pre-existing opinions. Hence, people are thought actively to seek out material that supports their opinions, and actively to avoid material that challenges them" (Sears and Freedman, 1967, 197). From this perspective, echo chambers are the outcome of deliberate choices. By contrast, the idea of "filter bubbles" centers the role of algorithms in producing such individualized spaces (Pariser, 2011). The mechanisms creating filter bubbles are largely invisible and operating without people's knowledge or explicit consent. Contrary to echo chambers, filter bubbles are therefore not entered voluntarily. Instead, they emerge as a side effect of the way in which the Internet works. Regardless of the specific mechanisms, both arguments posit that digital technology is conducive to homogenous online spaces in which people rarely meet contrasting view and, therefore, see their ideas affirmed and reinforced. Consequently, echo chambers and filter bubbles have been considered significant drivers of political polarization.

The arguments behind echo chambers and filter bubbles do not point unambiguously to a direct link between social media and ideological segregation online (Eady et al., 2019). While digital platforms increase choice as well as opportunities to self-select, or be selected by algorithms, into ideologically homogenous spaces, they also increase "incidental exposure," that is, the fact that users come across information they are not looking for, and specifically political information they disagree with, as well as political information in the first place (Feezell, 2018). People may use Facebook to catch up with their friends and watch funny videos, but in the process they may be exposed to news they would otherwise never see. Moreover, the sharing features of social media introduce a degree of ideological diversity. The ideology of content that users are exposed to via retweets is more moderate than that of tweets posted by users they follow (Eady et al., 2019).

The notion of "echo chambers" and "filter bubbles" has been very powerful in shaping popular understanding of the effects of digital technology on opinion formation and elections. However, like in the case of "fake news," research has increasingly challenged the empirical accuracy of these understandings, at least in their most extreme forms. As Barberá (2020, 39) puts it, "study after study demonstrates that despite citizens' ability to select the news stories they consume from a narrower range of sources thanks to digital technologies, they are nonetheless exposed to a diverse set of views through websites and even more so on social media." There are two main reasons why that is the case (Barberá, 2020). First, people are exposed to (political) content in a much more incidental, and less deliberate, way than previously assumed. Second, social media platforms connect people with other casual acquaintances ("weak ties") as much as close friends and family ("strong ties"). While "strong ties" tend to be ideologically homogenous, "weak ties" are not. Therefore, social media actually leads people to see a quite wide range of content because the connections with "weak" ties introduce a degree of ideological diversity that would otherwise be missing.

To study the effects of echo chambers and filter bubbles, a first set of works used an indirect strategy, exploiting exogenous variation in expansion of broadband internet access to establish a causal link between internet usage and political outcomes. In the US context, high-speed Internet was found to increase affective polarization (Lelkes et al., 2017), that is, the extent to which Americans dislike and distrust supporters of the other party (Iyengar et al., 2019). The study found that people are more likely to visit partisan media when they have access to broadband Internet, and that respondents with access to broadband Internet (instrumented by legislation facilitating its expansion) exhibit stronger partisan affect (Lelkes et al., 2017). Another study using data from Germany and Italy and broadband coverage as an instrument for online political news consumption concluded that internet access has a positive effect on support for populist parties (Schaub and Morisi, 2020). A similar study of the Italian case found that access to high-speed Internet initially decreased conventional political participation but later increased support for the protest Five-Star Movement (Campante et al., 2018).

These kinds of work can uncover the connection between internet access and political outcomes, but they are not designed to measure echo chambers or filter bubbles specifically. Another set of studies addresses the question more explicitly, using survey methodology. Overall, these studies have tended to confirm the view that echo chambers are not as pervasive as some fear. In a nationally representative UK sample, cross-cutting exposure was found to increase with the number of different news sources that respondents report consuming (Dubois and Blank, 2018). Survey data from the UK, USA, Germany, and Spain showed that respondents who find news via search engines access a wider range of online news, both regarding their number and their ideological diversity (Fletcher and Kleis Nielsen, 2018). A similar study comparing these countries plus Denmark and France found that respondents tend to read similar news media online and offline (although with some differences across countries), and that the degree of fragmentation of online and offline audiences is roughly the same, or smaller online than offline (Fletcher and Kleis Nielsen, 2018). A limitation of these kinds of studies is that they usually rely on self-reported measures of media consumption, which are not always reliable. However, the picture they paint is quite consistent and challenges the view that echo chambers are widespread among the public. Surveys have been used also to conduct experiments, either directly or by embedding environments meant to simulate social media platforms. This approach allows researchers to explore whether the specific mechanism through which social media increase cross-cutting (as opposed to selective) exposure is the visibility of "social endorsements," such as likes (Messing and Westwood, 2014). On the one hand, users may select content based on the source, which would reinforce selective exposure. On the other hand, users may rely on indicators of the popularity of content, which would increase the diversity of sources. Experiments revealed the power of such social endorsements, which turned out to be a stronger predictor of content selection than sources (Messing and Westwood, 2014). Furthermore, social endorsements more than compensate the selective exposure induced by source cues. On balance, in that study, social media increased the diversity of information to which users were exposed.

The unreliability of self-reported measures of behavior, common to traditional survey research, can be overcome by web-tracking data collected with the consent of users, which document what people actually do online, as opposed to they say they do. The web-browsing histories of 50,000 users in the US produced contradictory evidence on echo chambers (Flaxman et al., 2016). News accessed via social media or search engines is linked with higher ideological polarization compared to direct visits to news sites; however, cross-cutting content is over-represented in news obtained on social media or via search engines, because selective exposure is easier to achieve when people access known sources directly. Moreover, this study makes the important point that an overwhelming majority of news consumption takes place via direct visits to mostly mainstream media rather than social media or search engines, thus reflecting offline behavior. A large-scale multi-platform analysis demonstrated an increasing degree of similarity in the news sources consumed by the US online population, which is anchored by mainstream media, as well limited evidence for selective exposure along ideological lines (Yang et al., 2020). This conclusion is consistent with another study that found a low degree of political news consumption, a large overlap on the media diets of Democrat and Republicans, as well as higher election turnout among voters with the most conservative media diets (Guess, 2021). Therefore, although most citizens have moderate news consumption, those with extreme news engagement may be overrepresented among voters.

Web-tracking data have been used also outside the US context. Spanish data revealed that selective exposure is stronger when users access media sources directly and weaker when they reach them via Google searches, whereas Facebook is not directly linked to the degree to which users access sources in line with their ideological leanings (Cardenal et al., 2019). Like other studies, this research also finds a partisan asymmetry: exposure to cross-cutting content is higher among left-leaning than right-leaning individuals. However, different platforms matter in different ways for these groups (Cardenal et al., 2019). Facebook is associated with higher selective exposure among left-leaning users and lower selective exposure among right-leaning users (whence, probably, the null effects on average). For Google, on the other hand, the pattern is reversed. In the German context, results from large representative web-tracking datasets showed, first, that news are a small percentage of what users see online, and second, that the number of news visits, as well the number of different news sources, is positively related with usage of social media and search engines (Scharkow et al., 2020). These results indicate that online platforms foster rather than restrict varied online news consumption.

Another way to study echo chambers and filter bubbles without relying on self-reporting by users is to leverage social media data. This strategy allows researchers, for example, to consider not only what users read, or are exposed to, but also what they share. Twitter data showed that the degree of ideological segregation varies both across topics and partisan affiliations (Barberá et al., 2015). Content that is clearly political, such as discussions of election campaigns, tends to be shared within ideological clusters, whereas interactions on events that are less directly related to politics cut across ideological divides. Moreover, cross-ideological sharing is more likely for liberals than for conservatives. Overall, these findings suggest that echo chambers exist, but do not pervade on social media as a whole (Barberá et al., 2015).

Another study analyzed the Twitter accounts followed by a representative sample of Americans and found ambivalent evidence regarding echo chambers (Eady et al., 2019). First, about 40 percent of respondents do not follow any media sources, and about 50 percent no political accounts. This finding underscores how many users do not pay attention to hard news and politics. Second, among those users who do follow media accounts, there is a considerable overlap in the ideology of the sources they follow. At the same time, some sources (such as Fox News) that are very popular among conservatives do not reach liberals at all. Therefore, despite the significant common ground, there is a nontrivial amount of content that is consumed overwhelmingly by one group. Overall, Eady et al. (2019, 18) conclude they "do not find evidence supporting a strong characterization of 'echo chambers' in which the majority of people's sources of news are mutually exclusive and from opposite poles."

The role of algorithms in creating echo chambers is a key component of the filter-bubble argument, which is hard to study because it requires an uncommon degree of access to platform data. One of the few studies able to do so analyzed the behavior of millions of US Facebook users, and specifically how they interact with news shared on that platform (Bakshy et al., 2015). Results showed that while most friendships are within ideological groups, about one in five is cross-cutting, which leaves significant scope for exposure to ideologically diverse content. Moreover, engagements with cross-cutting content are driven primarily by user choices, not by algorithms. Those choices include, most importantly, the people that users befriend, but also the news users decide to engage with, once they have been exposed to it. Algorithms influencing the content of the news feed play only a subordinate role. The study concluded that "individual choices more than algorithms limit exposure to attitude-challenging content in the context of Facebook" (Bakshy et al., 2015, 1132). The data used in this work are of exceptional quality because they measure actual behavior. However, the results are necessarily constrained by the period in which the data were collected (2014–15). Social media platforms constantly tweak their algorithms, so it is hard to know to what extent the findings still apply today.

A YouTube study could confirm several findings from other research done on other platforms (Hosseinmardi et al., 2020). YouTube is a highly relevant platform, due its size (about 2 billion users), the role of algorithms in recommending content, and growing ideologically extreme content. The study found that most content viewed on YouTube is not news related, and most of the news is from mainstream or moderate sources. Second, algorithms likely play only a secondary role in exposures to radical content. Specifically, users reach far-right videos via different pathways in which YouTube recommendations play a minor role, and there is no trend toward more extreme content within viewing sessions suggesting that users actively seek out radical content. However, the study also found that radical-right content is growing on YouTube and that users who consume it tend to display a more extreme engagement pattern (Hosseinmardi et al., 2020).

While most studies using social media data, included those just discussed, conduct observational analyses, some could leverage the platforms to implement experiments. For example, one study addressed the idea that social media increase ideological polarization because they increase selective exposure and, conversely, reduce exposure to content going against preexisting views. The study randomly assigned Democratic and Republican Twitter users to content with the opposite ideological leaning (Bail et al., 2018). Contrary to expectations, exposure to cross-cutting content had little effect on Democrats and even made Republicans more conservative. These findings underscore that exposure to cross-cutting content as such may not be an adequate measure of polarization. Another randomized experiment assigned Facebook users recruited through a survey to receiving encouragements to like the pages of liberal or conservative media (Levy, 2021). These treatments increased the likelihood that they would see liberal or conservative news contents in their feeds. Results showed that exposure to counter-attitudinal news increases consumption. That is, if liberal (or conservative) users are randomly exposed to more content with a conservative (or liberal) slant, they also engage with those news items. In turn, such exposure has a negative effect on affective polarization (how much users dislike those of the opposite party) but has no effect on other political opinions. The study also showed that algorithms matter: liberals see more liberal news if they are randomly assigned to the liberal treatment than conservatives are, and vice versa. However, to the extent that users get to see news from a different ideological perspective, they are willing to engage with it, which decreases polarization. Overall, the findings support the view that filters tend to create bubbles, but they also show that such bubbles are by no means airtight.

2.3 Online Political Advertising

Online political advertising has become an appealing tool for political actors (Dommett, 2019). Online ads are substantially cheaper than other forms of advertising and, importantly, they promise much more precise targeting of the audience (Fowler et al., 2021, 132). That is, through online ads politicians can hope to reach very specific subgroups of voters and tailor their messages specifically for them. Moreover, in many countries online advertising is less regulated than other channels such as radio or TV due to loopholes in older legislation that failed to anticipate the importance of the Internet (Fowler et al., 2020). The widespread usage of online ads, coupled with the decentralized way in which advertising is purchased and the general lack of transparency (Fowler et al., 2020), has led to claims regarding their nature and effects. Online ads are often portrayed as incredibly sharp, allowing candidates to deliver the right kinds of message to the right kinds of people. However, these statements have been hard to verify independently from platforms or consultancy firms, because platforms usually do not grant researchers access to the data required to answer the question precisely. The Ad Library released by Facebook,[3] for example, includes only rough information on sociodemographic characteristics of the users who were exposed to the ads, but not on the features, possibly very fine-grained, that candidates actually selected for their targeting.

As a first step, it is useful to consider research on the effects of traditional political ads, which is much more extensive. The conclusion is that ads (as well as other forms of campaign contacts) generally have very small effects, if any. For example, a meta-analysis of field experiments found that ads fail to persuade voters to change their candidate choices (Kalla and Broockman, 2018). One concern is that the persuasive effects of ads may be heterogeneous, that is, zero on average but significant for some specific subgroups, but another meta-analysis confirmed that ads have small effects at best regardless of context, message, sender, or receiver (Coppock et al., 2020). Thus, the small average effects found in many studies are not primarily linked to heterogeneity. This is a relevant finding for online ads, given their capacity to fine-tune many aspects of the message. Of course, these conclusions cannot be directly extrapolated to online ads. Moreover, political ads may have effects other than persuasion, such as affecting media narratives (Kalla and Broockman, 2018, 150). However, the findings offer a useful baseline to understanding how online ads may

---

[3] www.facebook.com/ads/library/.

or may not work: changing people's mind is difficult, and absent solid evidence, claims that microtargeting or other forms of sophisticated ads may do so should be met with skepticism.

Despite the methodological challenges, several studies have begun to offer solid empirical evidence on the nature and consequences of online political advertising. A recent study uncovered several interesting facts in the US context (Fowler et al., 2021). Compared to TV advertising, Facebook ads are used by a much broader set of candidates. While TV ads are used extensively by more prominent politicians with greater resources, Facebook ads lower the barrier to entry and are accessible to any candidate, thus leveling the playing field to some extent. Moreover, geographic targeting seems to work. Relative to TV, Facebook ads are less likely to be seen by users outside the candidate's state. It should be noted, however, that this finding measures a kind of targeting that is much cruder than microtargeting, combining many characteristics of users, the effectiveness of which is hard to assess. Regarding the content of ads, Facebook differs significantly from TV. Facebook ads are less negative, less focused on issues, more partisan, and more segmented across sociodemographic groups. These findings suggest that Facebook ads aim to mobilize existing supporters rather than persuade undecided voters. Another study confirmed that the performance of ad targeting can vary significantly (Sances, 2019). The study compared the characteristics of groups targeted by ads as presented by Facebook, with the self-reported characteristics of respondents recruited using those ads. The comparison showed that accuracy varies drastically. While it is almost perfect (over 99 percent) for those characteristics that Facebook users self-report on their profiles, it can be as low as 24 percent for features that Facebook infers using statistical models and third-party data.

How effective are online targeted ads? In a commercial, nonpolitical context, targeting ads using psychological traits (extraversion and openness-to-experience) was found to increase clicks and purchases up to 50 percent (Matz et al., 2017). However, a limitation of the study design is that Facebook's optimization algorithms prevent reliable randomization of the ads, which biases the results (Eckles et al., 2018). Regarding political ads, one study examined the effects of targeting indirectly through a survey experiment among Latino voters in the USA (Ostfeld, 2017). The study randomized exposure to a Spanish version of an Obama campaign ad (compared to an English version) and found a positive effect on perceptions of Latino political in-group similarity, which might have increased turnout. Few studies could analyze the effects of targeted political ads directly. One such study randomized exposure to ads at the voting district level (Hager, 2019). That is, in this study, targeting is geographic, which is one of the biggest promises of online ads – showing ads only to people who can actually vote in a given election, or at least live in the relevant district. The study found positive effects of ads on party vote shares in the order of 0.7 to 2.2 percentage points. However, the estimates are imprecise (and not statistically significant) due to the relatively small number of areas subject to the experiment. Moreover, the study found minimal effects on turnout.

Another question is how many voters actually see political ads in the first place. Data from a YouGov panel of Facebook users based on desktop internet usage (that is, excluding mobile), revealed surprisingly low numbers (Guess, Lyons et al., 2019). During the weeks leading to the 2018 US midterm elections, 41.5 percent of respondents saw no ads at all, 12.8 percent one ad, and 18.8 percent between two and five ads. In other words, about a quarter (26.9 percent) of respondents were exposed to more than five ads. Moreover, the number of advertisers seen by respondents maps closely onto the number of impressions, which suggests that users were exposed to different ads and not repeatedly to the same ad. Although these findings should be replicated in other contexts, they offer a good baseline to assess claims regarding the prevalence of political ads online.

3 Political Participation

Political participation is a key element of democratic systems because it establishes a connection between the mass public and political elites (Kitschelt and Rehm, 2020, 318). Most generally, it can be understood as any citizen activity affecting politics (Van Deth, 2014, 351). The influential scheme advanced by Van Deth (2014) distinguishes between four categories: established forms of participation, such as voting and party membership; unconventional forms of participation aiming to influence political actors, such as protests and activism; activities aimed to specific problems or communities, such as civic engagement and volunteering; and forms of participation that originate in individual motivations, such as political expression. Moreover, the growing importance of digital technology has raised the question of the status of digital forms of participation, both conceptually and methodologically – for example, when designing surveys to measure participation (Theocharis, 2015; Theocharis and van Deth, 2018; Theocharis et al., 2021). This section discusses how digital technology has affected political participation in three key areas that are central in many taxonomies (e.g., Theocharis and van Deth, 2018), keeping in mind that "there is no unanimously agreed-upon typology of participatory practices" (Kitschelt and Rehm, 2020, 319). The three areas are voting, institutionalized participation (party membership in particular), and activism (including "digitally networked participation"). A fourth important area, civic participation, will be discussed in Section 4 because it overlaps significantly with aspects that are particularly salient in the policy-making context.

3.1 Voting

Voting is the most basic form of political participation and has been affected by digital technology in two direct ways: first, the option to vote online, and second, the availability of online tools designed explicitly to facilitate vote choices.

"Internet voting" refers to procedures in which voters cast ballots online and should be distinguished from other forms of electronic voting such as those relying on machines that replace the traditional ballot box (Alvarez et al., 2009, 497). The rationale of internet voting is primarily to make casting a ballot as easy as possible, matching the convenience people have come to expect from online shopping, online banking, and similar services. By improving convenience, internet voting may increase turnout, especially among groups that tend to vote at lower rates, such as younger voters, or for whom voting is cumbersome due to geographic distance (as for citizens living abroad) or other forms of physical restrictions (such as being quarantined during a pandemic) (Alvarez et al., 2009, 497). The effect of internet voting on political participation is one of the main normative questions associated with it. In general, more participation is good, but it depends on how it is distributed among different groups. If internet voting increases turnout especially among those citizens who already vote at higher rates (typically those with higher income and education), that would reinforce existing inequalities. In other words, the question is not just how internet voting affects turnout, but also political representation more broadly (Alvarez and Nagler, 2001).

Given the normative and practical relevance of the link between internet voting and participation, many studies aimed to assess how the availability of internet voting affects turnout in elections. One way to answer this question is to determine the profile of people who vote online. A study of eight elections in Estonia found that sociodemographic factors became less predictive of internet voting usage over time (Vassil et al., 2016). While early adopters of internet voting were younger and with higher degrees of digital literacy, the online channel was progressively used by a much wider range of people. These results do not imply directly that internet voting increases participation, but suggest that over time the tool becomes widespread among citizens and usage is not concentrated among particular types of voters. Another study in the Estonian context showed that internet voting may mobilize voters while having overall negligible effects on turnout (Vassil and Weber, 2011). The reason is that citizens who have a high propensity to vote (the majority of those who actually vote) turn out regardless of internet voting. By contrast, the availability of internet voting boosts participation among those voters who usually abstain, but the effect is not large enough to affect overall turnout significantly, given that abstainers tend to abstain even the presence of internet voting. Therefore, internet voting may counteract inequalities in political participation, but on a small scale. However, another study in the Estonian context found that internet voting is habit-forming at higher rates than paper voting (Solvak and Vassil, 2018). That is, first-time internet voters are more likely to keep voting online than first-time paper voters are to keep voting the traditional way, or that nonvoters are to keep abstaining. This finding suggests that the effects of internet voting on turnout may take a longer time to materialize, such that studies looking at turnout in a specific election may give an incomplete picture.

The evidence regarding overall limited effects of internet voting on turnout is quite consistent across countries. Switzerland is an interesting case because it has implemented pilots at the subnational level since the early 2000s, producing variations both across cantons and over time that researchers can leverage. Specifically, Germann and Serdült (2017) implemented a difference-in-differences design that helps to go beyond correlations and measure the causal effects of internet voting on turnout. In their analysis, the effects are indistinguishable from zero. It is important to note that postal voting is widespread in Switzerland, such that the added value of internet voting in terms of convenience is quite small. Another study in the Swiss context could leverage register data to study the effect of internet voting on turnout at the individual level (Petitpas et al., 2021). Results show that the availability of internet voting does increase turnout, but only for those people who are unlikely to vote in the first place. Coupled with small effect sizes (about 1.5 to 3 percentage points), the findings help explain why internet voting can have both a positive effect at the individual level and no measurable effect at the aggregate level – an argument that resonates with that of Vassil and Weber (2011) in the Estonian context.

Some of the most compelling results on the link between internet voting and turnout stem from a study of the Canadian province of Ontario, which revealed a positive 3.5 percentage-point effect on turnout on average, and twice as much in municipalities that did not use vote-by-mail (Goodman and Stokes, 2020). Therefore, the findings suggest that "there is likely a ceiling on how much convenience can increase turnout, and layering on additional convenience reforms likely boosts turnout by smaller additional margins, if at all" (Goodman and Stokes, 2020, 1164). This conclusion is consistent with Germann and Serdült (2017), which found little effect of internet voting in a context where vote by mail is widespread. Moreover, it is important to note that the 3.5 percentage-point estimate is based on local elections where the baseline participation rate is smaller than in national elections. Therefore, it is likely an upper bound of plausible effects of internet voting on turnout.

Another study conducted in the Canadian context gives additional evidence regarding the importance of convenience for the effects of internet voting on turnout. Some Canadian municipalities, however, switched completely to internet voting, which allows us to compare traditional paper voters and internet voters using survey data (Goodman et al., 2018). The study confirms the importance of sociodemographic factors and digital literacy for choosing internet voting when the option is offered in addition to paper voting. Moreover, the profile of internet voters is similar in cities that eliminated paper voting and in those that kept it as an option, which suggests that voters with lower degrees of digital literacy abstain when voting is possible only online. Although the elimination of traditional forms of voting is not on the agenda in most countries, these findings remind us that aggregate effects on turnout may hide inequalities between different groups of citizens.

Average effects of internet voting on turnout are important, but it is also important to understand how internet voting affects participation among different groups of citizens (Alvarez and Nagler, 2001). An important such group is expatriate voters, for whom the convenience value of internet voting is particularly high given the additional obstacles they face, such as longer trips to the embassy to vote or the potential unreliability of postal voting. Germann (2021) leveraged the temporary suspension of internet voting for Swiss citizens living abroad in 2015 and found a negative effect of the suspension on turnout of about five percentage points, in a context in which postal voting remained available. This effect size is comparable to that of other studies, such as Goodman and Stokes (2020), and suggests that internet voting has a meaningful but relatively modest impact on participation.

Another group for which internet voting may bring distinctive advantages are Indigenous people. In some Indigenous communities, many members live on off-reserve lands, which makes in-person participation difficult. Engagement is important to improve descriptive representation but also, more specifically, because in some countries, such as Canada, federal legislation requires that some participation thresholds are met to pass community laws (Budd et al., 2019). A case study of a First Nation community in Ontario found that internet voting is perceived as beneficial to community governance, and can be a tool to enhance self-determination (Budd et al., 2019).

In addition to turnout, a more technical, but very important concern with internet voting is security. Making sure that internet voting is secure has been challenging. In 2019, after decades of experimentation, a fatal flaw was found in the source code of the Swiss internet voting system, which was planned to be implemented nation-wide. Importantly, the problem could be detected because the Swiss government mandated the publication of the code, whereas New South Wales, in Australia, decided to keep the code secret although it was purchased by the same supplier as in Switzerland (Culnane et al., 2019). Public scrutiny is widely seen as a prerequisite for trust, especially when governments outsource development to private companies that may have incentives not to disclose security issues (Culnane et al., 2019; Park et al., 2021). Although security issues are the same in all countries, there is considerable variation in how internet voting is regulated. In the United States, the federal government sets voluntary standards; in Switzerland, it sets mandatory standards; in Canada, municipalities are largely free to implement their preferred solutions and what security measures they like, without necessarily having the resources to assess them (Essex and Goodman, 2020).

In a world where online shopping and banking are widespread, it might come as surprise that ensuring the security of internet voting is particularly challenging. There are several reasons why security issues are more critical for voting than for other sensitive online activities (Park et al., 2021). One reason is that online shopping and banking have a higher tolerance for failure. Fraud happens, but when it does, the risk is absorbed by companies as part of the cost of doing business. In contrast to elections, security problems usually do not raise to the systemic level. Moreover, the threat profile is more severe for elections, since it stems from nation-states instead of criminal organizations. This means that internet voting must be resilient to technically unsophisticated voters being attacked by the world's most sophisticated adversaries. Park et al. (2021, 1) concludes pessimistically that "online voting systems will suffer from such vulnerabilities for the foreseeable future given the state of computer security and the high stakes in political elections."

Beyond facilitating the act of voting itself, digital tools have also enabled new options for forming voting intentions, known as voting advice applications (VAAs). Like internet voting, VAAs promise to increase electoral participation – not by making voting more convenient, but by improving the information available to voters. VAAs are online platforms or apps that "assist voters in the electoral decision by comparing their policy preferences with the programmatic stances of political parties and/or candidates" (Marschall and Garzia, 2014, 1). Concretely, they require that users answer several policy questions that candidates have also previously answered, such that they can be matched. The output is usually a list or graph showing which party or candidate is closer to the user's preferences. VAAs are not inherently digital. The first were developed pre-Internet in the late 1980s, but their popularity increased when they moved online (Garzia et al., 2014). VAAs have been adopted in many countries; well-known examples include the German "Wahl-O-Mat" and the Swiss "smartvote," launched in 2002 and 2003, respectively (Marschall and Garzia, 2014, 2). Even though their immediate goal is to supply personalized information, VAAs are expected to have effects on political participation. In fact, improving representation is sometimes affirmed as an explicit goal. In this context, there are three main kinds of effects that may follow from VAAs: first, on the degree of information about politics and political parties; second, on participation in elections and, at the aggregate level, turnout; and third, on party and candidate choice (Marschall and Garzia, 2014, 5).

Although the effects of VAAs have been studied quite extensively, the findings are not always consistent. Early survey evidence from Switzerland showed that VAA users tended to be male, young, with higher education levels, above-average income, and above-average political interest and knowledge – in other words, they were not a representative sample of voters (Fivaz and Nadig, 2010). Forty percent of VAA users reported that the platform had some influence on their decision to vote, suggesting that it might have a positive effect in turnout. Moreover, the percentage was larger among women and young voters, two groups that tend to participate at lower rates. Two-thirds of users reported that the VAA had an impact on their vote choices and, women and young voters were more likely to agree with this statement. Moreover, about half of respondents who used VAA reported increased interest in looking for further information on particular candidates and parties, or politics in general. A related survey found that VAAs may appeal especially to low-propensity voters, specifically those who abstained in the previous elections rather than among those who reported participating (Ladner and Pianzola, 2010). A key limitation of these findings is that they are based on self-reported assessments by respondents who self-reported using VAAs. Still, they suggested that VAAs might be beneficial for political participation, in particular for voters who tend to participate less.

Although limited, these early findings tended to be confirmed by studies conducted in other contexts and with comparative data. Survey data from multiple European countries and elections between 2003 and 2013 revealed positive effects of VAA usage: between 1.8 and 16 percent for the probability of participation at the individual level, and between 0.7 and 6.3 percent for turnout at the aggregate level (Garzia et al., 2017). Importantly, these estimates rely on observational data and, therefore, cannot fully rule out that the effects are driven by unmeasured factors driving both VAA usage and participation. Testing the effects of VAAs experimentally in a real election setting is hard when VAAs are widely used. Such a context prevents a clear distinction between treatment and control groups, because voters who in the experimental setting are assigned to not using VAAs may still do so given their availability. An experiment conducted in Italy might avoid this problem because VAAs were not available at the time of research (Garzia et al., 2017). Respondents in the treatment group were encouraged to use a custom-made VAA that was not accessible to other people. The study revealed a positive effect of VAA of turnout on ten percentage points, which was driven in particular by individuals with a below-average propensity for voting, such as younger voters and women.

In addition to turnout, vote choice is another outcome that is potentially affected by VAA usage. This question was studied in a survey embedded in a VAA that was deployed during the 2009 European Parliament elections (Alvarez et al., 2014). European voters who decided to use the VAA were asked about their intended vote choice, both before and after seeing their match with different parties. The analysis was focused on the subset of users for which the VAA recommendation did not match the users' initial choice. The vast majority of such users did not change their preference despite seeing that a different party would be a better match. This suggests that the probability of switching is linked to the degree of "representative deficit," that is, the gap between a user's policy positions and those offered by the parties (Alvarez et al., 2014). The data support the view that VAA users are more likely to switch preferences if they are presented with alternatives that match their profile well. Like other VAA studies, a limitation is that the survey was opt-in and restricted to voters who self-selected into using the VAA. However, the results provide a useful benchmark for possible effects of VAA on party choice. The role of "representative deficit" for the impact of VAAs was further explored with a focus of turnout, instead of party choice, again in the context of the 2009 European Parliament elections (Dinas et al., 2014). The study found that the probability of abstaining increases when VAAs reveal to users that no party fits their preferences well. These findings indicate that VAAs can have a broader range of effects on participation: not only can they have a positive effect or no effect, but also a negative effect if voters learn that there is no party that is close enough to their preferences (Dinas et al., 2014). VAAs help align supply and demand, but if it turns out that the alignment is poor, users can be discouraged from voting.

At the level of voters, other relevant outcomes of VAA usage include political knowledge. Survey data from the 2009 German federal elections show that VAA usage is positively related to knowledge regarding the positions of political parties on 15 issues (Schultze, 2014). Moreover, VAA affect not only voters, but also parties (Garzia et al., 2014). Political parties may be involved in the selection and phrasing of the questions, and may be prompted to develop positions on issues that they previously paid little attention to, or to change their positions following the increased prominence of some issues in VAAs. Parties also need to pay attention to the coherence between their answers to VAA questions and the positions expressed in their manifestos, as well as between individual candidates. In some cases, parties may even attempt to disguise some of their positions in VAAs if they fear that they might be unpopular.

The endogeneity of VAA usage – the fact that VAA users and nonusers likely vary across many characteristics that are linked to both turnout and vote choice – is a significant issue that makes it difficult to estimate causal effects reliably. Some studies have attempted to address it using matching methods, to compare participation between VAA users and nonusers who are otherwise similar on many relevant dimensions. To the extent that the analysis considers all relevant predictors of both VAA usage and participation (which is not always a given in practice), such a procedure can improve estimates of causal effects. A study using this approach with data from the Netherlands, where VAA usage is widespread, concluded that the effect of VAA usage on turnout is about 4.4 percentage points (Gemenis and Rosema, 2014). Moreover, consistent with other studies, the effect is driven by individuals with a low propensity to vote, namely younger people, those with weak or no party identification as well as limited political knowledge. As discussed earlier, such effects are desirable from a normative perspective, since they stem from underrepresented groups. In this sense, VAAs may improve not just the quantity but also the quality of participation. These findings were corroborated using a similar matching approach and data from several Swiss elections (Germann and Gemenis, 2019). At the individual level, the effect of VAA usage on turnout was between 7.7 and 8.9 percentage points depending on the election, which translates to about 1.2 percentage points at the aggregate level. Moreover, the effects were larger among younger voters and those with lower education levels.

One of the few studies leveraging an experimental design to measure the causal effects of VAAs was conducted in Switzerland (Pianzola et al., 2019). Given that VAA usage is widespread, randomizing VAA usage is not feasible, because many individuals in the control groups will take advantage of VAAs anyway. Therefore, the study relied on an encouragement design where some people were alerted to VAAs and invited to use them. This approach generates exogenous variation in VAA usage that allows for causal inferences even though people in both the treatment and the control group end up using VAAs. Result showed that VAAs do have an effect on vote intentions (Pianzola et al., 2019). VAAs prompted voters to consider additional parties as alternative vote options, but at the same time ended up strengthening the initial choice. Munzert et al. (2021) relied on a similar encouragement design as Pianzola et al.

(2019), which however allows more precise measures of compliance, as well as additional outcomes, thanks to "trace data" such as web browsing. The study found that VAA usage has no effect on most outcomes: it does not increase (or decrease) turnout, vote choice, online news consumption, or political posts on social media (Munzert et al., 2021). It does, however, have a positive effect on issue knowledge, that is, which policy positions are supported by which parties. Moreover, the analysis revealed few differences in these effects across subgroups (such as younger voter or women), but it shows that respondents with lower levels of political knowledge and interest are least likely to use VAAs despite being encouraged to do so with monetary rewards. Munzert et al. (2021) conclude that VAAs do what they are supposed to do – improving political knowledge – but may fail to reach those voters who would most need a boost.

As we have seen, the literature on VAA is large and quite heterogenous in terms of research design and the kinds of outcomes that are considered. A meta-analysis covering fifty-five effects reported in twenty-two studies across nine countries reveals three key insights (Munzert and Ramirez-Ruiz, 2021). First, overall, the literature suggests that VAA usage has a positive effect on three key outcomes: turnout, vote choice, and political knowledge. Second, and importantly, the findings depend in no small part on the research design: the better studies account for self-selection, the smaller the effects. Experimental studies, which are best suited to deal with self-selection and measure causal effects, tend to find that VAA usage have no impact on turnout or vote choice. Third, political knowledge is an understudied outcome, although it is the main immediate goal of VAAs as well as, arguably, the outcome for which causal effects are the most plausible.

3.2 Institutionalized Participation

Digital technology has blurred the distinction between different forms of collective action, such as social movements and political parties. One of the most prominent examples is the Five-Star Movement in Italy, which not only relied heavily on digital platforms to create a movement and coordinate political action, but also integrated the "digital utopian" idea of the Internet as a self-organizing, disruptive platform into its worldview (Natale and Ballatore, 2014). The reliance on digital technology, combined with an emphasis on the expertise of common people, is one of the characteristics not only of the Five-Star Movement, but also of the Spanish Podemos and other parties that can be characterized as "techno-populist" (Bickerton and Accetti, 2018). In line with "digital utopianist" views, these parties aim to harness the collective intelligence of the web, and specifically of party members and sympathizers through some of the civic-tech instruments discussed in Section 4.2.

Digital technology has played different functions in the Five-Star Movement (Mosca, 2018). On the one hand, the Internet has served as a foundational myth, in which online participation makes it possible to realize the idea of direct democracy. On the other hand, the Internet has had a more practical purpose as an organizational tool. The Five-Star Movement's own platform was conceived to overcome hierarchies and the concentration of power, but in fact it is premised on interest aggregation through voting instead of discussion and deliberation (Mosca, 2018, 10). Until 2013, participation was limited to leaving comments on the movement leader's (Beppe Grillo) blog. New features were progressively introduced, first on the blog itself and later on a new platform designed for online participation, called Rousseau. The platform has two main functions: voting and proposing amendments to proposals elaborated by the movement's members of parliament. Regarding online votes, their usage decreased significantly between 2012 and 2017, with turnout dropping from over 60 percent to under 15 percent (Mosca, 2018). The trend was linked to a series of problems with the platform. Some of the issues are technical, such as concerns regarding the counting of votes and the transparency of the procedures. Others, however, were political. In particular, only the movement's leaders can determine the voting agenda as well as the timing of the vote; moreover, voters are strongly nudged toward the preferences of the leaders. The second function of the platform is the possibility to discuss draft legislation. Here, too, several problems have hampered engagement, such as the lack of specific procedures to structure debates and deal with user comments. Overall, a tension can be observed between the ideals that the platform is supposed to embody and the way it functions in practice, which is "more as a forum for discussion and evaluation than as a real online decision-making tool" (Mosca, 2018, 15). This tension is noted also by Stockman and Scalia (2020), who discuss additional problematic aspects of the Rousseau platform, such as the fact that (in contrast to the decidim platform in Barcelona, for example, discussed in Section 4.2) it runs on proprietary instead of open-source code and that it seems designed to prevent transparency and direct, horizontal communication among members.

The Five-Star Movement has been one of the most visible examples of how parties can leverage online platforms, but there have been others. The comparison with the German Piratenpartei shows how differences between platforms are linked to both ideological and organizational aspects (Deseriis, 2020). As discussed, the platform used by the Five-Star Movement is premised on the idea of the "general will" (hence the name, Rousseau) that is supposed to be revealed through plebiscitarian consultations. From this perspective, the emphasis on voting and the lack of tools for discussion and deliberation are therefore not bugs, but features, and the power of party leaders to control the agenda is consistent with these views. By contrast, the Piratenpartei proceeds from a very different assumptions – namely that of "liquid democracy" (hence the platform's name, LiquidFeedback) – that is, the idea, linked to public choice theory, that voters should be allowed to transfer their vote to other voters and even form longer delegation chains. At the organizational level, these two very different conceptions of the online platforms led to sharply contrasted outcomes: infighting in the Piratenpartei and centralization in the Five-Star Movement (Deseriis, 2020). While the usage of digital technology by parties such as the Five-Star Movement has disrupted traditional forms of organization, in other cases the change has been much more limited. In the German Green party, for example, online participation tools have not contributed to changing the power structure within the party, nor to expanding participation to new groups (Gerl et al., 2018). On the contrary, the members who were most active online are those who were already active.

3.3 Activism

Political participation goes well beyond conventional forms such as voting or engagement in formal decision-making processes. It includes unconventional forms such as protests and many other kinds of collective action aiming to advance political causes across the ideological spectrum. Beyond enabling existing forms of participation, digital technology may have generated a specific type of participation acts that are "more than just the online versions of offline political actions and thus a new type of behavior altogether" (Theocharis, 2015, 5). This form of participation has been labeled "digitally networked participation," defined as "a networked media-based personalized action that is carried out by individual citizens with the intent to display their own mobilization and activate their social networks in order to raise awareness about, or exert social and political pressures for the solution of, a social or political problem" (Theocharis, 2015, 6). Empirically, this kind of participation manifests itself primarily on social media, in the form of sharing political content, commenting on political or social issues, or calling for political action (Theocharis and van Deth, 2018; Theocharis et al., 2021).

Digitally networked participation, and online spaces more generally, have become particularly important for political activism (Theocharis et al., 2021). Research has challenged the proposition that social media only enable superficial and ineffective forms of political participation, sometimes described dismissively as "clicktivism" or "slacktivism" (Freelon et al., 2020). Online participation is a complement, not a substitute, for offline activism. For example, a meta-analysis of over a hundred studies found a strong positive connection between online and offline political engagement among youth (Boulianne and Theocharis, 2020). The connection can be problematic when it leads to violence: an analysis of twenty-five protests in the US and UK showed that the degree of violence tends to be higher when the events were preceded by intense and negative engagement among groups on Facebook (Gallacher et al., 2021).

One reason why online activism matters is that small acts of digital participation that are low-cost at the individual level may be consequential at the aggregate level (Margetts et al., 2016). Specifically, digital media afford two kinds of strategies: the first involves reaching online users directly, while the second leverages digital platforms to target traditional media. An important aspect is that left-wing and right-wing actors pursue these strategies to different degrees (Freelon et al., 2020). Activism on the left has relied on "hashtag activism," namely, the generation of awareness and support for progressive causes through slogans that spread from activist groups to mainstream media and the general public. At first, non-elite groups play a crucial role, but for the process to be successful the support of some elite actors is usually required. Conservatives, on the other hand, rely much less on the mainstream media, which they distrust. Instead, their online strategies involve a relatively self-contained media ecosystem that is used to reinforce partisan messages as well as spread disinformation (Freelon et al., 2020). (Disinformation and other forms of "fake news" are discussed more in detail in Section 2.1.)

The notion of "hashtag activism" contends that social media, and Twitter specifically, have empowered minorities and underrepresented groups to frame their grievances and claims autonomously, without being restricted by conventional narratives (Jackson et al., 2020). In the most successful cases, such efforts can reshape the political debate in ways that are advantageous to the activists and, potentially, prompt concrete policy actions. The best-known examples are probably #MeToo and #BlackLivesMatter, which originated in the US and have been influential at a global scale in reshaping the understanding of gender and racial equality, as well as #FridaysForFuture as a catalyst for worldwide protests for action against climate change. Another example is #MyNYPD, a hashtag that was used by non-elite members of marginalized communities to leverage a public relations campaign launched by the New York City Police Department in 2014. The hashtag was quickly hijacked to share photos of police violence, challenging the narrative that the NYPD was hoping to promote. Consequently, Jackson and Foucault Welles (2015, 936) identify Twitter as "a space that offers unique possibilities for public debate among activists, citizens, and media-makers seeking to define and redefine the role of the state in civil society." Another example of the ways in which Twitter can empower marginalized groups is the case of the hashtag #GirlsLikeUs (Jackson et al., 2018). The hashtag was used by the transgender community, particularly trans women, as a device for in-group solidarity but also to advocate for trans rights among the broader public. Taking stock of these and other studies, Jackson et al. (2020, 185) conclude that "Twitter represents a very real opportunity to work toward change by reintroducing and reframing issues for the public that have been either misrepresented or ignored in the mainstream public sphere."

At core, what hashtag activism does is creating and spreading new narratives to advance a given cause. But why are some narratives more successful than others? The nature of the messages is central, and specifically how they fit within preexisting discourses. An analysis of discussions on Facebook pages showed that users are more willing to engage with arguments advanced by activists when they are framed in an original way, connecting themes that are seldom discussed together (Bail, 2016). This insight might be helpful to explain why certain forms of hashtag activism succeed while others fail: it might depend to some degree on how the narratives manage to create innovative frames linking different perspectives.

Although hashtag activism can be very effective, it faces many challenges that can be illustrated with the case of #MeToo (Lindgren, 2019). Campaigns are hard to control and risk becoming noisy and diluted, because hashtags can be used in different and inconsistent ways. For example, #MeToo was progressively used in conjunction with many different topics, which lead to a diminished focus for the core message. Campaigns can also can produce pushback in the form of hate speech and trolling. In the case of #MeToo, tweets were initially very supportive of the cause but became increasingly antagonistic. Moreover, campaigns may lose momentum and face decreasing engagement, as illustrated by the fact that the number of retweets increased over time relative to original #MeToo tweets.

Hashtag activism is an example of what Margetts et al. (2016) have termed "chaotic pluralism," that is, the idea that one of the main consequences of social media for collective action is the increase of turbulence and unpredictability of political processes. The argument is twofold. On the one hand, digital platforms empower movements and groups that do not have access to traditional resources and institutions. This is the "pluralist" side of the argument. On the other hand, the kinds of collective action that emerge from this form of pluralism are "chaotic" in that they unfold from the aggregation of many actions that are initially small and largely uncoordinated – they are an emergent process that is hard to predict. A specific feature of digital media that facilitates this process is that social media make people's actions visible, and therefore helps to reveal preferences that would have previously remained hidden. This element affects the collective action capacity of different groups but in ways that are hard to predict, because it involves "a large number of failures and a small number of unpredictable, extreme events" (Margetts et al., 2016, 200). Another way to put it is that for each #BlackLivesMatter and #MeToo, there are thousands of hashtags that never take off, let alone have a concrete impact on politics and policy-making.

At the most general level, digital technology matters for collective action because of the "reconfigured logic of how and where we can interact; with whom; and at what scale and visibility" (Tufekci, 2017, 11). A key concern for activist groups, and social movements more broadly, is signaling their capacities to authorities in order to achieve their goals. Digital technology matters in ways that may or may not help social movements. A key dimension is "narrative capacity," that is, the "ability of the movement to frame its story in its own terms, to spread its worldview" (Tufekci, 2017, 192). As shown by Jackson et al. (2020) and others, social media have unique features that increase this capacity and make movements less dependent on traditional gatekeepers. However, on other dimensions, the effect of digital technology is more ambiguous. For example, digital technology massively increases the "disruptive capacity" of movements in the short term because it allows them to coordinate large-scale protests with very little planning. However, the spontaneous nature of the protests that digital technology enables – "adhocracy," as Tufekci (2017, 53) calls it – often becomes a liability when movements need to adapt their strategies to government responses. Moreover, mass protests with thousands of people in the streets may be a less credible signal of a movement's strength precisely because they do not require careful planning and organization. Therefore, Tufekci (2017, 269) concludes that "digital technologies can simultaneously empower movements and increase their capabilities but also complicate social dynamics, introduce new ones, and even fuel fragilities." Although these arguments are particularly salient in contexts with various degrees of repression, their relevance is not limited to particular political regimes.

4 Policy-Making

Like political communication and participation, policy-making is a key component of democratic politics. It is arguably one of the most constructive parts, because it involves, in principle, finding solutions to societal problems. A well-established model of the policy-making process is the policy cycle, which identifies several key stages: agenda setting, policy formulation, policy adoption, implementation, and evaluation (Knill and Tosun, 2020, 361). Digital technology has impacted most parts of the process. Starting with agenda setting, social media have provided new ways for political actors to increase the salience of certain issues as well as to influence how those issues are framed. This step is very important, because only a small subset of potential issues reaches the next stages in which potential solutions are discussed and enacted. In the policy formulation and adoption stages, digital technology has made it easier to crowdsource ideas and engage citizens with various kinds of "civic tech" tools. And in the implementation and evaluation stages, algorithms and other tools such as IT infrastructures have increasingly been used to inform, and hopefully improve, policy actions. Of course, the policy-cycle is a simple heuristic, such that the impacts of digital technology cannot always be assigned unambiguously to a specific stage. However, it can help us understand where they are situated within the policy-making process.

4.1 Agenda Setting

The first stage of the policy cycle involves the selection of issues that are considered on the political agenda, that is, "the list of issues to which political actors pay attention" (Walgrave et al., 2008, 815). The media play an important part in this process (McCombs and Shaw, 1993; Wolfe et al., 2013). In this regard, one of the most important structural changes of political communication induced by digital technology regards the shift of gatekeeping capacity away from traditional news media toward platforms, which affects how information is included or excluded from public discourse (Jungherr and Schroeder, 2021). These developments have both positive and negative consequences. On the one hand, social media contributes to greater pluralism, including voices that previously were excluded by traditional media – an argument that is relevant also for collective action, as discussed in Section 3.3. On the other hand, the public debate becomes more unstructured and includes extreme views that are potentially, and in some cases actually, dangerous. Moreover, while access to the platforms is mostly open, it is not enough to ensure reach. Voices need not only to be included, but also amplified, by platforms themselves, via algorithmic mechanisms, but also by traditional media (Jungherr and Schroeder, 2021).

To put it differently, digital platforms potentially have a significant impact on agenda-setting, that is, the process by which some issues receive political attention, while others do not. This is a classic concern in political science and public policy, going back at least to Schattschneider (1960) and Bachrach and Baratz (1962), who argued that the capacity to set the terms of the political debate – which issues are considered as political problems, and in which ways – is one of the most important forms of political power. It is also a classic concern for political communication research, which has long considered how the way in which the media frame issues affects public opinion (McCombs and Shaw, 1972, 1993). Social media and other platforms may significantly alter this process by reducing the power of traditional gatekeepers (political and media elites) to influence the salience of different issues as well as the frames used to discuss them, or, in other words, to "introduce, amplify, and maintain topics, frames, and speakers that come to dominate political discourse" (Jungherr et al., 2019, 17).

Gilardi et al. (2022b) identify three reasons why social media matter for political agenda setting. First, social media and other online platforms have become key channels for political communication (Jungherr, 2016). Second, beyond communication in general, social media matter for agenda setting specifically. As Lewandowsky et al. (2020, 2) put it, "the rapid rise of social media, including the microblogging platform Twitter, has provided new avenues for political agenda setting that have increasingly discernible impact." Similarly, Langer and Gruber (2020, 3) argue that "a thorough understanding of agenda setting necessitates a broadening of focus," including both traditional and social media. Third, a feature of "hybrid media systems" (Chadwick, 2017) in which traditional and social media coexist and interact with one another is that what happens on social media does not stay on social media. Instead, traditional media often amplify stories that first develop online, thus expanding their audience to people who do not necessarily consume digital media. It is well documented that journalists integrate social media in their reporting: "Tweets become public record and are increasingly incorporated into traditional journalistic coverage of political events" (Jungherr, 2014, 2). McGregor (2019, 1071) documents that "journalists draw on social media in various ways in the course of their reporting on political contests, from documenting public reaction to media events to evaluating the performances of candidates." Experimental evidence shows that journalists consider tweets as newsworthy as authoritative sources such as the Associated Press (McGregor and Molyneux, 2020). Furthermore, journalists tend to use tweets more as pieces of content rather than sources that need to be critically evaluated (Molyneux and McGregor, 2021). In turn, this practice contributes to legitimizing not only individual tweets, but Twitter as a whole as an authoritative source of information.

Empirical studies confirm the relevance of social media for political agenda setting. Barberá et al. (2019) consider the relationship between legislators and the public on Twitter, asking who leads and who follows in setting the agenda. The analysis shows that across a large number of issues, legislators tend to follow the public more than they lead it. There are some important differences, however. Legislators pay attention in particular to their own supporters (users who follow at least three legislators of the respective party), to a lesser extent to the "attentive" public (individuals who follow at least one major media outlet), and to an even smaller extent to the "general public" (users sampled regardless of following patterns). Another study focused on the relationship between political actors on social media (parties as well as individual politicians) and traditional media (Gilardi et al., 2022b). The analysis shows that issue salience on social and traditional media are closely linked and, overall, the social media agenda leads the traditional media agenda roughly to the same extent that it is led by it. These studies demonstrate the relevance of social media for agenda setting, but they also illustrate the extent to which social and traditional media are interconnected, in ways that are not easy to disentangle using observational data.

4.2 Crowdsourcing and Civic Tech

After agenda setting, the next step in the policy cycle is policy formulation. Here, digital technology plays an important role by increasing the number and kinds of people who can have a say in the decision-making process, and specifically in the elaboration of alternative policies. These forms of expanded decision-making facilitated by digital tools can be grouped in two related but distinct categories: crowdsourcing and civic tech. Succinctly, crowdsourcing is primarily an instrument with which decision-makers aim to improve policy formulation by integrating the inputs of many different people, whereas civic-tech puts a stronger emphasis on the value of participation as such, and often proceeds more bottom-up than crowdsourcing.

Crowdsourcing is a relatively broad notion, which "has come to be applied loosely to a wide variety of situations where ideas, opinions, labor, or something else is 'sourced' in from a potentially large group of people" (Lehdonvirta and Bright, 2015, 263). It takes several forms (Prpić et al., 2015; Taeihagh, 2017). Virtual labor marketplaces are commercial platforms such Amazon's MTurk where individuals are compensated for carrying out various kinds of tasks, such as classifying texts or images. Tournament crowdsourcing consists of competitions where individuals get a chance to win a prize by submitting ideas. Finally, open collaboration is a model in which organizations reach out to the public at large, and which does not involve material compensation.

In the context of policy-making, crowdsourcing refers to "new digitally enabled ways of involving people in any aspect of democratic politics and government, not replacing but rather augmenting more traditional participation routes such as elections and referendums" (Lehdonvirta and Bright, 2015,

263). The promise of crowdsourcing is that it "can give citizens an opportunity to have an impact on policies and even laws before institutional bodies, such as a local government or a national parliament, decide on them," specifically by encouraging citizens to work together online and generate new ideas (Aitamurto and Landemore, 2015, 1).

Crowdsourcing differs from traditional forms of citizen participation, such as referenda and petitions, in several ways. Crowdsourcing can be used to achieve several policy-making goals, such as empowering people by increasing their influence on solving public problems and increasing the effectiveness and legitimacy of policy-making (Liu, 2017, 2021), across different stages of the policy cycle, including the identification of problems, the development of ideas, drafting concrete proposals, decisions among alternatives, implementation, and the evaluation of policy outcomes (Aitamurto and Chen, 2017). How the inputs of the "crowd" are integrated into the decision-making process is flexible: they can be incorporated directly or play a subsidiary role in the form of advice, feedback, or benchmark (Liu, 2021). This is a major difference with referenda: while direct democracy transfers decision-making power from elected representatives to citizens, crowdsourcing pursues a participatory goal in which stakeholders (a group that is broader than voters) supply knowledge and information and are engaged throughout the policy-making process, thus providing "epistemic value" – that is, "discovering knowledge that would otherwise remain unknown," reaching beyond groups that are traditionally involved in decision-making processes (Aitamurto and Chen, 2017, 60). In other words, the goal of crowdsourcing is to gather information, expertise, and experiences instead of opinions; it is "not merely a better form of opinion polling or aggregating preferences, but a way to bring collective intelligence to bear to solve problems" (Alsina and Martí, 2018, 339). Moreover, technology plays a distinctive role. Not only does it make possible and convenient for individuals to participate, it also helps to aggregate the knowledge generated in the participation process.

Concretely, crowdsourcing projects usually take place in an online platform to which users are invited to participate by policy-makers. It is important to recognize that, most of the time, users are a strongly self-selected sample that is not representative of the broader population. This is not problematic insofar as the goal of crowdsourcing "is not to create a mini-public" (Aitamurto and Chen, 2017, 68). Instead, "crowdsourcing has no target group defined ex ante" (Aitamurto and Landemore, 2015, 2). Nonetheless, it can be a diverse set of people including groups that are underrepresented in traditional participation channels such as elections, or may be excluded due to a lack of voting rights. Ideally, crowdsourcing is transparent, increases knowledge about policies and decision-making processes, can reach a large and diverse set of users thanks to its online tools, and fosters open and free exchanges with deliberative elements. If these conditions are fulfilled, a case can be made that crowdsourcing has positive democratic value (Aitamurto and Chen, 2017). In practice, several factors influence the success of crowdsourcing projects (Liu, 2017). It depends not only on whether the goals are defined clearly, but also on whether the advantages of crowdsourcing over traditional processes have been articulated. Moreover, the crowdsourcing process should take into account both the capacities and the incentives of participants. Material considerations such as prizes or monetary rewards are important, but the intrinsic motivation of participants also matters and is linked to opportunities for learning and skill building. Finally, peer-review mechanisms and reputation systems can also improve the quality of the work done by participants.

Aitamurto and Landemore (2015) identify five normative principles for crowdsourced policy-making, which are summarized in Table 3. Three (inclusiveness, accountability, and transparency) are criteria that apply to democratic processes more in general, while two (modularity and synthesis) are specific to crowdsourcing. First, the inclusiveness principle implies that the process should include a large number of people from diverse backgrounds, to ensure both the legitimacy and the efficacy of the process, since a heterogenous group is more likely to see problems from different perspectives relevant for policy solutions. The importance of inclusiveness is underscored also by the notion of "collective intelligence," that is, "the general ability of the group to perform a wide variety of tasks" (Woolley et al., 2010, 687), on which crowdsourcing is premised. Importantly, collective intelligence is "a property of the group itself, not just the individuals in it" (Woolley et al., 2010, 687). An important question is therefore how the composition of the crowd affects the performance of the work it does. Hong and Page (2004, 16385) demonstrate that, given a large pool of potential participants, diversity in "how people represent problems and how they go about solving them" is even more important than individual expertise or ability. Using the case of Wikipedia, Shi et al. (2019) show that ideologically diverse groups produce higher-quality content, not only on political topics but more generally. The reason is that diverse groups engage in more thorough discussions, taking more perspectives into account. This insight underscores how crowdsourcing projects in the policy-making context should take care to represent a wide range of political views, even in cases where the issues are not particularly controversial. From a practical perspective, in crowdsourcing a first step toward inclusiveness is accessibility. That is, crowdsourcing projects should be highly visible with low barriers to entry. It should be as easy as possible for anyone to participate. The second normative principle identified by

Table 3 Principles for crowd sourced policy-making (adapted from Aitamurto and Landemore, 2015, 9).

Principle	Goal	Process	Design
Inclusiveness	Involvement of people from a diversity of backgrounds	Communication strategy to maximize attention	User-friendliness, low barriers for participation
Accountability	Justification of authorities' decisions to the public	Communication with participants	Tools for communication both among participants and with authorities
Transparency	Ability to understand the process	Communication with participants	Tools for peer-to-peer communication
Modularity	Comprehensibility of a complex policy-making process, possibility of both ad-hoc and long-term participation	Organization of the process in meaningful sequences, modules, and tasks	Visualization of organization steps and status of process
Synthesis	Explanation of outcomes	Steps for collecting, summarizing, and sharing crowd's inputs with the public	Tools for automatized analysis of inputs

Aitamurto and Landemore (2015) is accountability, which posits that the initiators of the crowdsourcing project should communicate clearly how the project is structured and provide feedback to users at each step. Users should know whether the expectations were fulfilled and be informed about the decisions and courses of action taken. The third principle, transparency, means that users (as well as anyone else) should understand how the crowdsourcing project is embedded in the broader policy-making process. Fourth, the modularity principle stems from the fact that policy-making processes can take a long time. Therefore, the crowdsourcing project should be split into several stages so that participants do not feel lost or overwhelmed. Fifth, the synthesis principle means that the information generated by the crowd should be summarized and linked to specific outcomes.

Similar to crowdsourcing, civic tech is a relatively loose concept. It can defined as "technology that is explicitly leveraged to increase and deepen democratic participation" (Gilman, 2017, 745). Therefore, it differs from crowdsourcing, in that it is not simply a tool that authorities can use to gather information and increase the legitimacy of decisions. Instead, civic tech is a more strongly bottom-up approach that aims to change the traditional relationship between citizens and the state. Through its focus on participation, civic tech is linked to the notion of collaborative governance, which highlights institutional arrangements that foster citizen engagement in policy-making (Gilman, 2017). The particular feature of civic tech is that such engagement is fostered through new digital tools.

One of the earliest and most widespread forms of civic tech is participatory budgeting, that is, "a program in which the government (usually local) invites residents to make decisions on the city budget, in whole or in part. It is then up to the residents to suggest, discuss, and nominate projects that can be carried out within the proposed budget" (Barros and Sampaio, 2016, 296). Participatory budgeting was originally applied in the Brazilian city of Porto Alegre in 1989 and then spread within Brazil as well as internationally. The first online projects date back to the early 2000s. They aimed to expand participation, which in some cases reached tens of thousands of people, for example, over 170,000 in Belo Horizonte (Barros and Sampaio, 2016, 293). A crucial component for the success of participatory budgeting initiatives is citizen satisfaction with the process. In Belo Horizonte, participation decreased sharply after allegations of fraud, lack of engagement from the authorities, and failure to implement the projects selected by citizens (Barros and Sampaio, 2016).

In Europe, Spanish cities have been pioneers in the area of participatory budgeting and civic tech more generally (Smith and Martín, 2020). The platforms used in Madrid ("Decide") and Barcelona ("Decidim") are open source and

Table 4 Functions of civic tech platforms (based on Smith and
Martín, 2020, 7).

Citizen debates	Initiate debates on any topic
Citizen proposals	Propose policies
Citizen budgets	Propose and vote on how budget should be spent
Citizen plans	Participate in development of urban plans

have been adopted by many other cities. Although their specific features vary, they typically include those shown in Table 4. Proposing and voting on budgets are just one of the functions. Citizen can also use the platforms to conduct debates on any issue they want, to propose specific policies, and to participate in urban planning. It thus becomes apparent how such platforms can potentially enhance citizen participation in many different ways. The options have been used quite extensively in Madrid and Barcelona. In Madrid, for example, after four years there were over 655,000 users registered on the platform, who created over 27,000 proposals, initiated over 5,600 debates and received over 200,000 comments, and cast over 4 million votes (Smith and Martín, 2020, 7).

The Spanish experience teaches several useful lessons (Smith and Martín, 2020). First, although their success required a favorable political context, the platforms were developed bottom-up by "technopolitical" activists, not by authorities. Second, and consistent with their activist origins, the platforms adopted an open source, noncommercial approach. Third, the platform needed to be integrated within official institutional channels, which created several frictions. Decisions made on the platforms depend on political and administrative support either for enactment or implementation. Therefore, proposals may be applied slowly, or not at all. Fourth, the platforms have increasingly relied on gamification techniques (such as intermediary milestones or awards) to keep citizens engaged. However, gamification does not solve the problem of mobilizing citizens in the first place. To motivate citizens to participate, platforms must respond to citizens' needs and show that participation is consequential, which is not always the case due to implementation problems. To mobilize participation, offline activities are often required. Finally, the platforms have been used also for meta-discussions regarding the design, use, and governance of the platforms themselves.

Civic tech is related to the notion of participatory governance, that is, "participatory forms of political decision making, involving organised and non-organised citizens, to improve the quality of democracy" (Bua and Bussu, 2020, 1). There are different forms of such participation, which vary depending on how top-down and institutional versus bottom-up and transformative they are. Specifically, Bua and Bussu (2020) contrast "governance-driven democratization" and "democracy-driven governance." In the former model, citizen participation is a way to improve the legitimacy and effectiveness of policy-making by including more voices and sources of information. The latter, by contrast, is closely linked to social movements and other forms of collective action attempting to create new forms of participation. What both forms have in common is the attempt to embed participation within established institutions such as public administration. That is, both forms leverage existing rules and process and can therefore be contrasted with the forms of participation discussed in Section 3.3.

4.3 Big Data and Algorithmic Decision-Making

Moving further along the policy cycle, a key way digital technology matters is how big data and algorithms have been increasingly used to inform both policy formulation and implementation. The idea that digital technology may help government actors be more efficient and make better decisions is not new, and constitutes a paradigmatic shift following the demise of New Public Management – the reliance on market mechanisms into public administration – in the mid-2000s (Margetts and Dunleavy, 2013). The integration of digital tools in policy-making promised several benefits, including the automatization processes that are cumbersome for humans and the improvement of services with new ways to respond to to the needs of citizens and businesses (OECD, 2005). The promises have been lofty: the combination of "artificial" intelligence and "collective" intelligence (crowdsourcing) has been heralded as a way to anticipate citizens' needs, preempt problems through improved forecasting, and analyze large amounts of citizen data and feedback (Verhulst et al., 2019).

The goals that big data may help pursue in policy-making can conflict with the public values involved in their different usages, such that a number of trade-offs emerge (Ingrams, 2019). For example, the value of equal treatment of citizens may go against the kinds of personalized public service delivery that big data make possible. Similarly, the value of privacy may conflict with transparency, but also with effectiveness to the extent that big data are employed to address problems using personal information such as trace data. As shown in Table 5, each goal of big data can be linked to specific values on two dimensions, technocratic and citizen. First, "data management" refers to technical infrastructure to manage big data for public policy. On the one hand, this goal is based on the technocratic values of effectiveness and efficiency, which may contrast with some citizen values such as privacy, but be in line with others such as openness. Second, "personalization" involves tailoring service

Table 5 Big data in policy-making: Goals and public values (adapted from Ingrams, 2019, 134)

	Goals of big data in policy-making			
	Data management	Personalization	Problem-solving	Productivity
Technocratic values	Effectiveness Efficiency	Effectiveness Efficiency Consumer focus	Effectiveness Efficiency	Efficiency
Citizen values	Privacy Openness	Privacy Equality	Privacy Openness Equality	Privacy Legitimacy

delivery to the specific needs of individual users. In addition to effectiveness and efficiency, a third technocratic value in this context is consumer focus. These values may be in conflict with the citizen value of privacy, since individualized services rely on detailed information on users. Similarly, consumer focus may contrast with equality. The third goal, "problem solving," is focused squarely on efficiency and effectiveness. Depending on the specific applications, there may be a tension with equality, for example, when algorithms reproduce existing inequalities or create new ones, as well as privacy, when personal information is collected. On the other hand, the goal of "problem-solving" may foster openness when citizens are more strongly involved in decision-making processes. Finally, "productivity" is about increasing efficiency, which may improve the "output legitimacy" of policy-making, but also contrast with privacy like the other goals, since big data are inherently problematic for data protection.

One of the most important developments has been the integration of big data and algorithms into decision-making processes. In this context, algorithmic decision-making is a broad notion that "refers to the use of algorithms as an aid or as a substitute to human analysis, to make or inform (and improve the quality of) decisions or actions" (Busuioc, 2020, 4). In this context, the term "algorithm" is used loosely to describe a wide range of computer programs that are used to analyze data, spanning from conventional statistical methods to cutting-edge machine learning and artificial intelligence applications. Figure 3 shows how different kinds of inputs can be used for various applications thanks to particular functions enabled by algorithms. Inputs are varied and may include sensors, text, images, video, speech, and sound. Algorithms can work

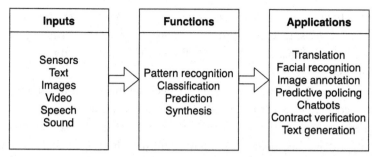

Figure 3 Inputs, functions, and applications of algorithms in policy-making
(adapted from Christen et al., 2020, 73)

with these sources to carry out different kinds of tasks, such as pattern recognition, classification, prediction, and summarizing information. In turn, these functions are useful for many different applications, for example, facial recognition tools that the police may use to identify suspects, predictive policing (e.g., estimating the probability of various kinds of risks), the programming of chatbots for automated responses to citizen's inquiries, or automatized control of contracts or tax records. These applications promise not only efficiency and speed, but also substantively better decisions. For example, an algorithm could improve integration outcomes for refugees by up to 40% in the USA and Switzerland by optimizing their resettlement to specific regions based on historic data (Bansak et al., 2018).

Despite their potential and, in some cases, demonstrated benefits, it is important to recognize that the performance of algorithms varies considerably and may not always be up to the expectations set by the companies that sell them. For instance, the accuracy of a commercial algorithm widely used to predict recidivism in the criminal justice context was shown to be no better than that of nonexperts recruited through the crowdsourcing platform Amazon's Mechanical Turk (Dressel and Farid, 2018). Moreover, a well-known problem is that reliance on algorithms may introduce various kinds of bias, including discrimination based on gender, race, or religion (Buolamwini and Gebru, 2018). Algorithms learn from the data that are fed to them, including the prejudices associated with different kinds of groups (Williams et al., 2018). If the outputs of the models are taken at face value, decisions are likely to reproduce existing biases in society and reinforce discrimination patterns under the appearance of objectivity. Other problems are linked to the opacity of algorithms (the fact that they often work as black boxes) as well as the automation of decision-making, that is, the limited role of human input (Zarsky, 2016; Danaher et al., 2017). In conjunction, these issues may limit the effectiveness of algorithmic decision-making. The general difficulty of predicting human behavior is exacerbated by the limitations of the datasets that are used. Furthermore, there are questions related to fairness, given that different groups could be advantaged or disadvantaged in ways that are arbitrary, difficult to understand, and not based on explicit consent.

A key issue for the use of algorithmic decision-making in the public sector is accountability, that is, the requirement that decisions are justified and that there are consequences in case of misbehavior. There are several reasons why algorithmic decision-making may contrast with accountability requirements (Busuioc, 2020). First, the fact that many algorithms, especially the most sophisticated ones, operate as black boxes, collides with the first requirement of accountability, namely, that one can understand how decisions are made. The problem is compounded by the fact that many algorithms, including those used in the public sector, are proprietary. Understanding how algorithms make decisions is difficult even if the code is open source, but is almost impossible if it is kept private. Second, accountability requires not only that decisions are transparent, but also that the rationale behind decisions is explained and justified. This requirement introduces an additional set of complications, including the fact that, in most cases, decisions do not derive from algorithms directly, but from the interaction of algorithmic outputs and human decision-making. This aspect can be problematic in itself, for example, if algorithmic and human biases reinforce each other in ways that are hard to assess (O'Neil, 2016; Eubanks, 2018). Finally, accountability requires consequences in case of failure, which is difficult when decisions are not transparent and cannot be justified and, therefore, cannot be meaningfully contested by those negatively affected by them. However, this should not be an argument for public administration to avoid responsibility (Busuioc, 2020, 9). Instead, the burden is on the public sector to adopt tools that are compatible with accountability requirements. These arguments resonate with calls for using "simpler" models in cases of high-stakes decisions, that is, models that are "inherently interpretable" (Rudin, 2019). At the same time, some scholars have argued holding algorithmic decision-making to a higher standard than human decision-making would be a mistake: people are biased, too, and their decision-making process is not necessarily more transparent than that of algorithms (Zerilli et al., 2019). Furthermore, the use of algorithms, if properly regulated (for example regarding data availability and code transparency) might make discrimination more detectable compared to human decision-making (Kleinberg et al., 2020). A key reason is that proof of discrimination is typically provided at the aggregate level in terms of statistical patterns, not at the level of individual decision-making responsible for discriminatory choices. Demonstrating the discriminatory intentions of specific organizations or individuals is very hard, and arguably harder than in the case of algorithms, which "by their nature require a far greater level of specificity than is usually involved with human decision making" (Kleinberg et al., 2020, 30096). For example, Arnold et al. (2021) put forward an approach to detect racial discrimination in algorithmic bail decisions. Although the method relies on nontrivial requirements such as quasi-random assignment of decision-makers, it shows how algorithms lend themselves to additional layers of scrutiny beyond what is possible for human decision-making.

Many issues with algorithmic decision-making arise from its technical features, but it is also important to understand how its appeal and limitations are perceived by those using the tools (Hartmann and Wenzelburger, 2021). In high-stakes contexts such as criminal justice, the appeal of algorithms to decision-makers is that they help to reduce uncertainty by transforming it into statistical risk. As discussed earlier, decision-makers may over-rely on algorithms and take predictions or estimates at face value even when they are based on questionable assumptions or data. From the decision-maker perspective, another appeal of algorithms is that they may help them shift the blame for wrong decisions away from them selves and toward technical tools. Although Hartmann and Wenzelburger (2021) do not find direct evidence for blame shifting in their case study, due to the normatively unappealing nature of blame shifting it is possible that decision-makers downplay its role, either consciously or unconsciously.

A critical aspect of algorithmic decision-making is that the combination of artificial intelligence and the large amounts of data that required to make it work opens the door for new or increased forms of surveillance. These fears are particularly acute in autocratic states but are not limited to them. In a case study of the Los Angeles Police Department, Brayne (2017) identifies several dimensions that are likely to apply in other contexts. For example, algorithmic decision-making increases the degree to which individual risk assessment is quantified and reduces the degree of discretion left to human input. Moreover, it affects the scale of surveillance, in that predictive policing can be deployed at the level of neighborhoods or other geographic units. Passive, systematic surveillance is facilitated at a large scale via alert systems instead of active queries in databases that require human input. Through large-scale data collection systems, a larger number of individuals end up in law enforcement databases, including people who have not had any contact with the police and who would otherwise have escaped surveillance. Finally, data sources that were previously separated can be merged, which increases the amount of data the police have access to. These elements may reproduce existing inequalities (O'Neil, 2016; Brayne, 2017; Eubanks, 2018; Benjamin, 2019). On the one hand, the reliance

on data and algorithms may reinforce surveillance on people already under sus-
picion under a coat of objectivity that, as discussed earlier, may be misleading.
On the other hand, it can broaden the scope of individuals that can be monitored.

5 Digital Technology as a Political Problem

This Element has discussed how digital technology affects liberal democracies in three key areas: political communication, political participation, and
policy-making. This concluding section takes stock of the previous sections
in two ways. First, it maps out the areas where there is a research consensus
as well as gaps in our knowledge. Second, it elaborates on the link between
"problems" and "solutions" in the area of digital technology and politics,
and specifically on the importance of the problem-definition stage of policy-
making to understand ongoing attempts to design regulatory responses to the
perceived challenges of digital technology. The section concludes by arguing that while policy-making efforts in this area are hampered by significant
gaps in our knowledge regarding the nature of the problem induced by digital
technology, they are equally constrained by an increasing degree of political contestation even in areas that are supposedly technical—and that these
kinds of political contestation are themselves subject to the influences of digital
technology.

5.1 What We Know, What We Don't

Political communication is the area in which the role of digital technology
has been most researched from a social science perspective, on the one hand
because it has been a long-standing focus of communication scholars, and on
the other hand because of its salience among policy-makers, journalists, and the
general public following Donald Trump's election in 2016. However, it is not
necessarily the area where we know the most or, more precisely, where there
is the strongest consensus regarding basic facts and relationships (much less
causal effects). The reason is that the impact of digital technology on political
communication is the domain that is most affected by the research challenges
described in Section 1.2 with the metaphor of a sand castle: hard to construct,
and quick to decay. A partial consensus exists that the most extreme claims
regarding the spread and effects of misinformation, echo chambers, and filter
bubbles are not supported by empirical evidence. Most people are not significantly exposed to "fake news," they do not live in echo chambers, and the
effects of social media on political polarization and election outcome are likely
relatively small and indirect (though probably not negligible). Frustratingly,
researchers struggle to produce more precise answers due to the lack of data

access as well as the constantly changing political communication ecosystem. The fact that most research is based on the specific case of the United States is an additional limitation.

Compared to political communication, our knowledge of the link between digital technology and political participation stands on firmer ground. There is a consensus that internet voting is not a game changer, meaning that its effects on political participation are rather limited and conditional on the broader institutional context (in particular, the convenience of voting using established channels, which is not necessarily the same for all voters). At the same time, internet voting raises security challenges that remain unresolved. The open political question concerns the desirability of online voting channels given the security problems and limited (but nonzero) benefits for political participation. Regarding institutionalized participation, specifically in political parties, digital technology does have the potential to transform the relationship between party basis and elites. Interestingly, the outcomes depend in part on the specific technology adopted, which may lead to centralization (in the case of the Movimento 5 Stelle in Italy) or on the contrary disorganization (in the case of the German Piratenpartei) when more radical approaches are adopted. By contrast, more incremental steps may have little effect. From both a social science and political perspective, the most dynamic area is that of activism, where research has shown that social movements and advocacy groups have used digital technology to advance their causes by leveraging the affordances of social media to change public discourse on issues such as gender and racial equality. From a broader perspective, an ongoing debate has concerned the conceptual status of digital acts of participation. The notion of "digitally networked participation" (Theocharis, 2015) posits that they constitute a new form of participation instead of an extension of existing ones, which has consequences for the ways political participation is researched, notably using surveys.

Turning to policy-making, the field is quite heterogeneous and fragmented. Research on agenda setting has shown the relevance of social media for shaping the issues policy-makers care about, but suffers from some of the same limitations of political communication studies in terms of data access and rapidly changing ecosystems, such that findings remain tentative. Civic tech and crowdsourcing is a domain that has not been sufficiently studied from an empirical social science perspective. There is a gap between the promises advanced by both activist and developers and actual evidence regarding their benefits for policy-making, for example, in terms of inclusiveness as well as quality of the decision-making process. Algorithmic decision-making is one of the most exciting and important areas. Like for civic tech and crowdsourcing, there is still much to learn about the actual performance of AI tools in a policy-making context. At the same time, the potential drawbacks are clear. On the one hand, there is a demonstrated danger of bias and discrimination against particular groups, particularly when algorithms are used uncritically. On the other hand, algorithmic decision-making can infringe on privacy and data protection, given that AI necessarily requires large amounts of data to be collected, processed, and classified. Consequently, it is not surprising that this is one of the areas in which there have been active regulation efforts. Finally, e-government is an area in which the impact of digital technology is most visible from the point of view of citizens, but which is relatively dull from a social science angle. The benefits of digitizing administrative process are undisputed, and the drawbacks relatively limited and straightforward (for example, ensuring accessibility). The biggest challenges stem from the implementation of e-government strategies within public administration, which can be fruitfully approached from organizational perspectives.

Stepping back to consider the big picture, the diversity of the matter stands out. Digital technology affects democratic politics in all its components; however, each part tends to be examined in specific literatures that are typically unrelated. A fully integrated approach is not realistic, and probably not even desirable given the need for specialization. Different questions require different approaches, which face different challenges. The "sand castle" problem affects many areas, but not all, and not to the same extent. That said, a greater awareness of the many aspects of the connection between digital technology and politics would be highly beneficial, because in some cases a higher degree of engagement across subfields would be meaningful. First, the importance of social media is not limited to political communication; it pervades the whole democratic process, including political participation and policy-making. In this context, a more integrated perspective would be helpful and its development might be facilitated by the connections highlighted in this Element. Second, there is a sharp divide between the widely shared notion that digital technology is causing new "problems," and the ways in which those problems are framed and, consequently, the kinds of solutions that are advanced to address them. We turn to this question in the next section.

5.2 From Problems to Solutions

The headline "Congress agrees big tech creepy, can't agree how," shown in Figure 2, illustrates a fundamental point. There is a widely held view that digital technology causes problems requiring policy responses, but there is no consensus on what the problems actually are, nor, therefore, what kinds of actions would be appropriate. Even the agreement on the root cause might be misguided to the extent that "digital technology is seen as the driver of trends that have deeper, more longstanding, and social and institutional roots" (Barrett et al., 2021). There is nothing special about this tension. Disagreement about the nature of problems and solutions is a key feature of politics (Schattschneider, 1960; Bachrach and Baratz, 1962). As Green-Pedersen and Walgrave (2014, 7) write, "politics is about problems – not in the sense of being a matter of rational responses to objective problems, but in the sense of how conditions become political problems to which politicians try to deliver solutions." Only a small fraction of issues are treated as politically relevant problems. Moreover, *how* issues are framed matters a great deal. Because "policy problems are not a priori givens but rather are matters of definition . . . what is at issue in the agenda-building process is not just which problems will be considered but how those problems will be defined" (Elder and Cobb, 1984, 115). Such definitions are crucial for the kinds of policies that are adopted; this assertion is considered "nearly axiomatic" (Boushey, 2016, 200). Therefore, to different degrees, "problem definition" permeates every policy-making process. However, it is particularly significant in the area of digital technology, for two reasons. First, policy-makers often struggle to fully understand the issues: "Governments are typically not entirely aware of the nature of the policy problem they are trying to address and are unsure of what a regulatory solution might look like" (Taeihagh et al., 2021, 3). This fact is due to the information asymmetry between policy-makers and tech companies, compounded by the challenges academic researchers are confronted with when studying the effects of digital technology, as discussed in Section 1.2. Second, problem definition in this area is subject to a high degree of political contestation enabled by digital technology itself. Social media have boosted the collective action capacity of political activists, especially those supporting progressive causes (Section 3.3), and traditional gatekeepers such as party and media elites can be bypassed, which makes it possible for different kinds groups to influence the political agenda (Section 4.1). A full explanation of the link between problems and solutions in the area of digital technology and politics is beyond the scope of this Element. Instead, the rest of this section illustrates the importance of the question in two cases: content moderation and artificial intelligence.

Content moderation refers to the practice of screening and monitoring content posted by users on social media sites to determine if the content should be published or not, based on specific rules and guidelines (Gillespie, 2018). It sounds like a narrow issue, but it is central to online political communication (Section 2). Examples include the filtering of illegal content on social media (such as copyrighted or pedopornographic materials) but also anything that goes against the relatively vague community standards of the platforms.

Content moderation has far-reaching technical, legal, and political implications that create both pressure and challenges for public and private regulation (Gillespie, 2018). From the perspective of most users, content moderation is barely visible and, to the extent it is, appears fully automatized. However, there are many humans in the loop, workers located all over the world who are paid to constantly screen content (Roberts, 2019). Still, algorithms play a central and increasingly essential role. Due to the scale of the problem – hundreds of millions of pieces of content to be screened every day – content moderation has become unmanageable without the assistance of automatized tools. Algorithmic moderation relies on two sets of approaches: matching and classification (Gorwa et al., 2020). Matching involves the comparison of "hashes" (digital fingerprints) to determine if two pieces of content are the identical or very similar. A typical application is the detection of copyright infringement, for example, for videos uploaded to YouTube. Classification, by contrast, aims to determine whether a piece of content falls into a given category, such as hate speech or nudity.

These systems do not work flawlessly but are constantly improving. However, regardless of their technical performance, they raise several political issues, such as the lack of transparency regarding decision-making rules, unequal impacts across different groups, and the depoliticization of fundamental normative issues such as the definition of "terrorism" or "hate speech" (Gorwa et al., 2020). Therefore, content moderation is by far not a strictly technical problem. It raises major legal conundrums, especially regarding the principle of free speech in the US context (Douek, 2021a). Traditionally, free speech problems have been approached from a perspective focusing on specific pieces of content. However, the scale of the problem has rendered this approach unfeasible. Another active legal debate concerns the merits of international human rights law as a guidance for content moderation, which has been advocated by some academic and civil society groups, but whose effectiveness remains disputed (Douek, 2021b). On top of technical and legal issues, the most intractable problems are political, and involve balancing the costs and benefits of content moderation, as well as determining how public or private actors should regulate it. Any content moderation policy must come to terms with the fact that some lawful speech may, and likely will, be suppressed along with unlawful speech (Keller, 2018). That can be an unintended consequence of stricter rules: when faced with potentially severe consequences for infringements, platforms will err on the side of over-removal (Douek, 2020). Due to these inherently political issues, many agree that content moderation rules should not be left entirely to platforms, but a real alternative to self-regulation has not emerged yet. In the "governance triangle" with states, NGOs, and firms at the vertices

(Gorwa, 2019), content moderation rules are currently a mix that is predominantly shaped by firms. Facebook's Oversight Board, which made its first decisions in 2021, including high-profile cases such as Trump's ban, is an example of the increasing formalization of self-regulation in this area (Klonick, 2020).

The case of content moderation shows how the policy-making process is still in the problem-definition and agenda-setting stages. Although it raises key questions regarding the regulation of the public sphere, which is a key element of democratic politics (Figure 1), content moderation became a politically salient issue only recently, when social media platforms started to take a more active stance toward prominent politicians, specifically Donald Trump. An analysis of the social media discourse showed that the number of tweets on content moderation took off after Twitter started fact-checking Donald Trump's tweets in June 2020, and reached a peak when Facebook and most other platforms decided to ban Donald Trump following the Capitol riot on January 6, 2021 (Alizadeh et al., 2022). Moreover, the frames used to discuss the issue vary across ideological groups. In particular, right-wing users were more likely than left-wing users to link content moderation with Section 230, the part of the United States Communications Decency Act that protects social media companies from liability for the content that is published on their sites, while at the same time granting them freedom to moderate content. Indeed, US policy-makers have increasingly focused on repealing or revising Section 230 as a way to address content moderation, even though the protection it grants to social media companies arguably encourage them to take a less restrictive stance.[4] In sum, the "problem" of content moderation, and the "solutions" advanced to address it, are increasingly subject to political contestation, including in online spaces.

Turning to *artificial intelligence*, machine learning and related technologies are a key component of algorithmic decision-making, which we discussed in Section 4.3, but to different degrees AI permeates most of the areas discussed in this Element, and indeed of society in general (Burrell and Fourcade, 2021). Therefore, it is not surprising that its regulation has become a key question for both public sector organizations and private companies. The ethics of AI is an area where the need for action is widely recognized, and where both public and private actors have attempted to develop rules to ensure that the usage of AI does not lead to unintended negative consequences such as the discrimination of certain groups. While there is a consensus that rules are needed, no agreement exists on question such as "which ethical principles should be prioritized

---

[4] www.nytimes.com/2021/03/09/technology/section-230-congress.html.

and how conflicts between ethical principles should be resolved" (Jobin et al., 2019, 396). This heterogenous approach to AI regulation reflects the scope and diversity of AI applications as well as of the issues that they raise, which call for a differentiated approach. One way to approach the problem is to think about the role of AI in decision-making in terms of principal-agent relationships (Krafft et al., 2020). Principal-agent relationships are common in many social and political contexts. They derive from the asymmetry of incentives and information between a "principal," who delegates some tasks, and the "agent" to whom the tasks are delegated (Miller, 2005). The application of ideas to the AI regulation helps to think about how decisions made or supported by algorithms (the "agent") may conflict with the interests of the people or groups for whom or about which the decisions are made. The conflict may originate from diverging objectives (resulting, for example, from implicit assumptions or data quality) or information asymmetries (due to the "black box" nature of AI). To counter these problems, Krafft et al. (2022) map different mechanisms with different degrees of stringency onto a space with two dimensions: the scope for "agency loss" and the intensity of potential harm. When both are low, mild forms of regulation linked to market mechanisms might be sufficient; as their degree increases, more robust forms are required; and in extreme cases where both agency losses and potential harm are severe, the prohibition of algorithmic decisions might be taken into consideration. The European Union has been at the forefront the regulation of AI. In April 2021, the European Commission put forward a proposal that promises to become the first set of binding rules on AI globally and might become influential beyond the EU's jurisdiction (European Commission, 2021). In particular, the proposed legislation distinguished between three categories of AI depending on their degree of risk, which it links to rules with different stringency, including bans for the most risky usages (Burri and von Bothmer, 2021). At the same time, risk is defined relatively narrowly, such that most uses of AI will be lightly regulated, if at all. Given these challenges, the regulation of AI is bound to remain an important area of policy-making for years to come.

Debates surrounding "AI ethics" – "the principles and values that should guide its development and use" (Jobin et al., 2019, 389) – and its implications for regulatory demands are an example of online political contestation in the area of digital technology. Specifically, the commitment of private companies to improve the ethics of AI has been questioned as shallow and potentially counterproductive in that it might prevent stronger public regulation. Recent controversies surrounding Google's ethics in AI work, notably in the context of the firing of researcher Timnit Gebru in December 2020, have taken place on social media under hashtags such as #ISupportTimnit, #AIethics, and

#MakeAIEthical. The protests have focused especially on the limited progress that Google and other tech companies have made in the areas of diversity and inclusion, and these protests have reached the mainstream media.[5] Whether and how these online movements will affect policy-making is an open question, but the example illustrates an important point: the "problem" of digital technology and politics is in the process of being defined, and that process is shaped by digital technology itself.

5.3 Conclusion

The digital transformation of politics and policy-making is real and here to stay. The impact of digital technology permeates the entire political process, affecting the flow of information among citizen and political actors, the connection between the mass public and political elites, and the development of policy responses to societal problems. Some elements are specific to some parts of the process; for example, internet voting comes with a distinct set of security challenges that are largely irrelevant in other areas. By contrast, social media play a key role throughout the process, from the spread of information and disinformation, to enabling new forms of political participation, to shaping how issues receive attention on the policy-making agenda. What is also common throughout the process is the view that digital technology raises new problems, as well as the lack of consensus on how to address them. In no small part, the confusion regarding policy responses is linked to the difficulty of producing a precise diagnosis of the disease. Due to the lack of access to platform data, independent researchers have struggled to determine the precise extent of online disinformation, much less its consequences on opinions and behavior. Without established facts, policy-makers are left with insufficient empirical guidance. However, it would be a mistake to reduce the disorientation of policy-makers to a shortage of reliable information. As in any area, problems are not a given; instead, they are subject to political contestation. How problems are understood, or framed, determines the solutions that are elaborated to address them, and indeed whether policy-makers consider that a solution is needed in the first place. In other words, not only problem definition matters, but the problem-definition stage, I argue, is the stage that currently matters most at the intersection of digital technology, politics, and policy-making. By shedding light on these questions, scholars have the chance of making a real contribution beyond academic research. Hopefully this Element will be a useful resource toward this goal.

---

[5] E.g., www.nytimes.com/2021/03/15/technology/artificial-intelligence-google-bias.html.

References

Aitamurto, T. and K. Chen (2017). The value of crowdsourcing in public policymaking: Epistemic, democratic and economic value. *The Theory and Practice of Legislation 5*(1), 55–72.

Aitamurto, T. and H. E. Landemore (2015). Five design principles for crowdsourced policymaking: Assessing the case of crowdsourced off-road traffic law in Finland. *Journal of Social Media for Organizations 2*(1), 1–19.

Alizadeh, M., F. Gilardi, E. Hoes, K. J. Klüser, M. Kubli, and N. Marchal (2022). Content moderation as a political issue: The Twitter discourse around Trump's ban. Working paper, University of Zurich.

Allcott, H. and M. Gentzkow (2017). Social media and fake news in the 2016 election. *Journal of Economic Perspectives 31*(2), 211–236.

Allen, J., B. Howland, M. Mobius, D. Rothschild, and D. J. Watts (2020). Evaluating the fake news problem at the scale of the information ecosystem. *Science Advances 6*(14), eaay3539.

Alsina, V. and J. L. Martí (2018). The birth of the crowdlaw movement: Tech-based citizen participation, legitimacy and the quality of lawmaking. *Analyse & Kritik 40*(2), 337–358.

Altay, S., E. de Araujo, and H. Mercier (2020). "If this account is true, it is most enormously wonderful": Interestingness-if-true and the sharing of true and false news. Digital Journalism, http://doi.org/10.1080/21670811.2021.1941163.

Altay, S., A.-S. Hacquin, and H. Mercier (2020). Why do so few people share fake news? It hurts their reputation. *New Media & Society* (forthcoming).

Alvarez, R. M., T. E. Hall, and A. H. Trechsel (2009). Internet voting in comparative perspective: The case of Estonia. *PS: Political Science and Politics 42*(3), 497–505.

Alvarez, R. M., I. Levin, P. Mair, and A. Trechsel (2014). Party preferences in the digital age: The impact of voting advice applications. *Party Politics 20*(2), 227–236.

Alvarez, R. M. and J. Nagler (2001). The likely consequences of internet voting for political representation. *Loyola of Los Angeles Law Review 34*, 1115–1153.

Aral, S. (2020). *The Hype Machine: How Social Media Disrupts Our Elections, Our Economy, and Our Health – and How We Must Adapt*. New York: Currency.

Arnold, D., W. Dobbie, and P. Hull (2021). Measuring racial discrimination in algorithms. *AEA Papers and Proceedings 111*, 49–54.

Bachrach, P. and M. S. Baratz (1962). Two faces of power. *American Political Science Review 56*(3), 947–952.

Bail, C. A. (2016). Combining natural language processing and network analysis to examine how advocacy organizations stimulate conversation on social media. *Proceedings of the National Academy of Sciences 113*(42), 11823–11828.

Bail, C. A., L. P. Argyle, T. W. Brown et al. (2018). Exposure to opposing views on social media can increase political polarization. *Proceedings of the National Academy of Sciences 115*(37), 9216–9221.

Bail, C. A., B. Guay, J. Maloney et al. (2020). Assessing the Russian Internet Research Agency's impact on the political attitudes and behaviors of American Twitter users in late 2017. *Proceedings of the National Academy of Sciences 117*, 243–250.

Bakshy, E., S. Messing, and L. A. Adamic (2015). Exposure to ideologically diverse news and opinion on Facebook. *Science 348*(6239), 1130–1132.

Bansak, K., J. Ferwerda, J. Hainmueller et al. (2018). Improving refugee integration through data-driven algorithmic assignment. *Science 359*(6373), 325–329.

Barari, S., C. Lucas, and K. Munger (2021). Political Deepfake Videos Misinform the Public, But No More than Other Fake Media. https://osf.io/cdfh3/

Barberá, P. (2020). Social media, echo chambers, and political polarization. In N. Persily and J. A. Tucker (eds.), *Social Media and Democracy: The State of the Field, Prospects for Reform*, pp. 34–55. Cambridge: Cambridge University Press.

Barberá, P., A. Casas, J. Nagler et al. (2019). Who leads? Who follows? Measuring issue attention and agenda setting by legislators and the mass public using social media data. *American Political Science Review 113*(4), 883–901.

Barberá, P., J. T. Jost, J. Nagler, J. A. Tucker, and R. Bonneau (2015). Tweeting from left to right: Is online political communication more than an echo chamber? *Psychological Science 26*(10), 1531–1542.

Barrett, B., K. Dommett, and D. Kreiss (2021). The capricious relationship between technology and democracy: Analyzing public policy discussions in the UK and US. *Policy & Internet*, 13(4), 522–543.

Barros, S. A. R. and R. C. Sampaio (2016). Do citizens trust electronic participatory budgeting? Public expression in online forums as an evaluation method in Belo Horizonte. *Policy & Internet 8*(3), 292–312.

Bauer, P. C. and B. C. von Hohenberg (2020). Believing and sharing information by fake sources: An experiment. *Political Communication*, 38(6), 647–671, http://doi.org/10.1080/10584609.2020.1840462.

Baumgartner, F. R. and B. D. Jones (1993). *Agendas and Instability in American Politics*. Chicago: University of Chicago Press.

Benjamin, R. (2019). Assessing risk, automating racism. *Science 366*(6464), 421–422.

Benkler, Y. (2020). A political economy of the origins of asymmetric propaganda in American media. In W. L. Bennett and S. Livingston (eds.), *The Disinformation Age: Politics, Technology, and Disruptive Communication in the United States*, pp. 43–66. New York: Cambridge University Press.

Benkler, Y., R. Faris, and H. Roberts (2018). *Network Propaganda: Manipulation, Disinformation, and Radicalization in American Politics*. New York: Oxford University Press.

Bickerton, C. J. and C. I. Accetti (2018). "Techno-populism" as a new party family: The case of the Five Star Movement and Podemos. *Contemporary Italian Politics 10*(2), 132–150.

Boulianne, S. and Y. Theocharis (2020). Young people, digital media, and engagement: A meta-analysis of research. *Social Science Computer Review 38*(2), 111–127.

Boushey, G. (2016). Targeted for diffusion? How the use and acceptance of stereotypes shape the diffusion of criminal justice policy innovations in the American states. *American Political Science Review 110*(1), 198–214.

Branch, J. (2021).What's in a name? Metaphors and cybersecurity. *International Organization*, 75(1), 39–70.

Brashier, N. M., G. Pennycook, A. J. Berinsky, and D. G. Rand (2021). Timing matters when correcting fake news. *Proceedings of the National Academy of Sciences*, 118(5), e2020043118.

Brashier, N. M. and D. L. Schacter (2020). Aging in an era of fake news. *Current Directions in Psychological Science 29*(3), 316–323.

Brayne, S. (2017). Big data surveillance: The case of policing. *American Sociological Review 82*(5), 977–1008.

Bruns, A. (2019). After the "APIcalypse": Social media platforms and their fight against critical scholarly research. *Information, Communication & Society 22*(1), 1544–1566.

Bua, A. and S. Bussu (2021). Between governance-driven democratisation and democracy-driven governance: Explainingx changes in participatory governance in the case of Barcelona. *European Journal of Political Research*, 60(3), 716–737.

Budd, B., C. Gabel, and N. Goodman (2019). Online voting in a First Nation in Canada: Implications for participation and governance. In R. Krimmer,

M. Volkamer, V. Cortier, B. Beckert, R. Küsters, U. Serdült, and D. Duenas-Cid (eds.), *Electronic Voting*, pp. 50–66. New York: Springer International Publishing.

Buolamwini, J. and T. Gebru (2018, Feb 23–24). Gender shades: Intersectional accuracy disparities in commercial gender classification. In S. A. Friedler and C. Wilson (eds.), *Proceedings of the 1st Conference on Fairness, Accountability and Transparency*, Volume 81 of *Proceedings of Machine Learning Research*, pp. 77–91. New York: Proceedings of Machine Learning Research.

Burrell, J. and M. Fourcade (2021). The society of algorithms. *Annual Review of Sociology 47*, 213–237.

Burri, T. and F. von Bothmer (2021). The New EU Legislation on Artificial Intelligence: A Primer. https://papers.ssrn.com/sol3/papers.cfm?abstract_id=3831424

Busuioc, M. (2021).Accountable artificial intelligence: Holding algorithms to account. *Public Administration Review* 81(5), 825–836.

Campante, F., R. Durante, and F. Sobbrio (2018). Politics 2.0: The multifaceted effect of broadband internet on political participation. *Journal of the European Economic Association 16*(4), 1094–1136.

Cardenal, A. S., C. Aguilar-Paredes, C. Galais, and M. Pérez-Montoro (2019). Digital technologies and selective exposure: How choice and filter bubbles shape news media exposure. *The International Journal of Press/Politics 24*(4), 465–486.

Carlson, M. (2020). Fake news as an informational moral panic: The symbolic deviancy of social media during the 2016 US presidential election. *Information, Communication & Society 23*(3), 374–388.

Chadwick, A. (2017). *The hybrid media system: Politics and power*. Oxford: Oxford University Press.

Christen, M., C. Mader, J. Čas, et al. (2020, February). *Wenn Algorithmen für uns entscheiden: Chancen und Risiken der künstlichen Intelligenz*. Zürich: Hochschulverlag AG.

Clayton, K., S. Blair, J. A. Busam, et al. (2020). Real solutions for fake news? Measuring the effectiveness of general warnings and fact-check tags in reducing belief in false stories on social media. *Political Behavior 42*(4), 1073–1095.

Coppock, A., S. J. Hill, and L. Vavreck (2020). The small effects of political advertising are small regardless of context, message, sender, or receiver: Evidence from 59 real-time randomized experiments. *Science Advances 6*(36), eabc4046.

Culnane, C., A. Essex, S. J. Lewis, O. Pereira, and V. Teague (2019). Knights and knaves run elections: Internet voting and undetectable electoral fraud. *IEEE Security Privacy 17*(4), 62–70.

Danaher, J., M. J. Hogan, C. Noone, et al. (2017). Algorithmic governance: Developing a research agenda through the power of collective intelligence. *Big Data & Society 4*(2), 1–21.

Deseriis, M. (2020). Digital movement parties: A comparative analysis of the technopolitical cultures and the participation platforms of the Movimento 5 Stelle and the Piratenpartei. *Information, Communication & Society 23*(12), 1770–1786.

Dinas, E., A. H. Trechsel, and K. Vassil (2014). A look into the mirror: Preferences, representation and electoral participation. *Electoral Studies 36*(C), 290–297.

Dommett, K. (2019). The rise of online political advertising. *Political Insight 10*(4), 12–15.

Douek, E. (2020). The rise of content cartels. New York: Knight First Amendment Institute at Columbia University.

Douek, E. (2021a). Governing online speech: From 'posts-as-trumps' to proportionality and probability. *Columbia Law Review 121*(3), 759–833.

Douek, E. (2021b). The limits of international law in content moderation. *UC Irvine Journal of International, Transnational, and Comparative Law 6*(1).

Dragu, T. and Y. Lupu (2021). Digital authoritarianism and the future of human rights. *International Organization 57*.

Dressel, J. and H. Farid (2018). The accuracy, fairness, and limits of predicting recidivism. *Science advances 4*(1), eaao5580.

Dubois, E. and G. Blank (2018). The echo chamber is overstated: the moderating effect of political interest and diverse media. *Information, Communication & Society 21*(5), 729–745.

Eady, G., J. Nagler, A. Guess, J. Zilinsky, and J. A. Tucker (2019). How many people live in political bubbles on social media? Evidence from linked survey and Twitter data. *SAGE Open 9*(1), 215824401983270–21.

Eckles, D., B. R. Gordon, and G. A. Johnson (2018). Field studies of psychologically targeted ads face threats to internal validity. *Proceedings of the National Academy of Sciences of the United States of America 54*, E5254–E5255.

Egelhofer, J. L. and S. Lecheler (2019). Fake news as a two-dimensional phenomenon: A framework and research agenda. *Annals of the International Communication Association 43*(2), 97–116.

Elder, C. D. and R. W. Cobb (1984). Agenda-building and the politics of aging. *Policy Studies Journal 13*(1), 115–129.

Esser, F. and B. Pfetsch (2020). Political communication. In D. Caramani (ed.), *Comparative Politics* (5th ed.), pp. 336–358. Oxford: Oxford University Press.

Essex, A. and N. Goodman (2020). Protecting Electoral Integrity in the Digital Age: Developing E-Voting Regulations in Canada. *Election Law Journal 19*(2), 162–179.

Eubanks, V. (2018). *Automating inequality: How high-tech tools profile, police, and punish the poor*. London: St. Martin's Press.

European Commission (2018). A multi-dimensional approach to disinformation: Report of the independent high level group on fake news and online disinformation. Brussels, Publications Office, 2018, https://data.europa.eu/doi/10.2759/0156.

European Commission (2021). Fostering a European approach to Artificial Intelligence. COM(2021) 205 final.

European Data Protection Supervisor (2020, January). A preliminary opinion on data protection and scientific research. Brussels: European Data Protection Supervisor, pp. 1–36.

Farrell, H. (2012). The consequences of the Internet for politics. *Annual Review of Political Science 15*, 35–52.

Feezell, J. T. (2018). Agenda setting through social media: The importance of incidental news exposure and social filtering in the digital era. *Political Research Quarterly 71*(2), 482–494.

Fivaz, J. and G. Nadig (2010). Impact of voting advice applications (VAAs) on voter turnout and their potential use for civic education. *Policy & Internet 2*(4), 167–200.

Flaxman, S., S. Goel, and J. M. Rao (2016). Filter bubbles, echo chambers, and online news consumption. *Public Opinion Quarterly 80*(S1), 298–320.

Fletcher, R. and R. Kleis Nielsen (2018). Automated serendipity: The effect of using search engines on news repertoire balance and diversity. *Digital Journalism 6*(8), 976–989.

Fowler, E. F., M. M. Franz, G. J. Martin, Z. Peskowitz, and T. N. Ridout (2021). Political advertising online and offline. *American Political Science Review 115*(1), 130–149.

Fowler, E. F., M. M. Franz, and T. N. Ridout (2020). Online political advertising in the united states. In N. Persily and J. A. Tucker (eds.), *Social Media and Democracy: The State of the Field, Prospects for Reform*, pp. 111–138. Cambridge: Cambridge University Press.

Freelon, D. (2018). Computational research in the post-API age. *Political Communication 35*(4), 665–668.

Freelon, D., A. Marwick, and D. Kreiss (2020). False equivalencies: Online activism from left to right. *Science 369*(6508), 1197–1201.

Freeze, M., M. Baumgartner, P. Bruno, et al. (2020). Fake claims of fake news: Political misinformation, warnings, and the tainted truth effect. *Political Behavior*.

Fung, A., H. Russon Gilman, and J. Shkabatur (2013). Six models for the internet + politics. *International Studies Review 15*(1), 30–47.

Gallacher, J. D., M. W. Heerdink, and M. Hewstone (2021). Online engagement between opposing political protest groups via social media is linked to physical violence of offline encounters. *Social Media+ Society 7*(1), http://doi.org/10.1177/2056305120984445.

Garzia, D., A. H. Trechsel, and A. De Angelis (2017). Voting advice applications and electoral participation: A multi-method study. *Political Communication 34*(3), 424–443.

Garzia, D., A. H. Trechsel, K. Vassil, and E. Dinas (2014). Indirect campaigning: Past, present and future of voting advice applications. In B. Grofman, A. H. Trechsel, and M. Franklin (eds.), *The Internet and Democracy in Global Perspective*, pp. 25–41. New York: Springer.

Gemenis, K. and M. Rosema (2014). Voting advice applications and electoral turnout. *Electoral Studies 36*(C), 281–289.

Gerl, K., S. Marschall, and N. Wilker (2018). Does the Internet encourage political participation? Use of an online platform by members of a German political party. *Policy & Internet 10*(1), 87–118.

Germann, M. (2021). Internet voting increases expatriate voter turnout. *Government Information Quarterly 38*.

Germann, M. and K. Gemenis (2019). Getting out the vote with voting advice applications. *Political Communication 36*(1), 149–170.

Germann, M. and U. Serdült (2017). Internet voting and turnout: Evidence from Switzerland. *Electoral Studies 47*, 1–12.

Gilardi, F., L. Baumgartner, C. Dermont, et al. (2022a). Building research infrastructures to study digital technology and politics: Lessons from Switzerland. *PS: Political Science & Politics*, 55(2): 354–359.

Gilardi, F., T. Gessler, M. Kubli, and S. Müller (2022b). Social media and political agenda setting. *Political Communication*, 39(1), 39–60.

Gillespie, T. (2018). *Custodians of the Internet: Platforms, content moderation, and the hidden decisions that shape social media*. New Haven, CT: Yale University Presss.

Gilman, H. R. (2017). Civic tech for urban collaborative governance. *PS: Political Science and Politics 50*(3), 744–750.

Gohdes, A. R. (2020). Repression technology: Internet accessibility and state violence. *American Journal of Political Science*, 64(3), 488–503.

Goodman, N., M. McGregor, J. Couture, and S. Breux (2018). Another digital divide? Evidence that elimination of paper voting could lead to digital disenfranchisement. *Policy & Internet 10*(2), 164–184.

Goodman, N. and L. C. Stokes (2020). Reducing the cost of voting: An evaluation of internet voting's effect on turnout. *British Journal of Political Science 50*(3), 1155–1167.

Gorwa, R. (2019). The platform governance triangle: Conceptualising the informal regulation of online content. *Internet Policy Review 8*(2), 1–22.

Gorwa, R., R. Binns, and C. Katzenbach (2020). Algorithmic content moderation: Technical and political challenges in the automation of platform governance. *Big Data & Society 7*(1).

Green-Pedersen, C. and S. Walgrave (2014). Political agenda setting: An approach to studying political systems. In C. Green-Pedersen and S. Walgrave (eds.), *Agenda Setting, Policies, and Political Systems: A Comparative Approach*, pp. 1–16. Chicago, IL:: University of Chicago Press.

Grinberg, N., K. Joseph, L. Friedland, B. Swire-Thompson, and D. Lazer (2019). Fake news on twitter during the 2016 US presidential election. *Science 363*(6425), 374–378.

Guess, A., J. Nagler, and J. Tucker (2019). Less than you think: Prevalence and predictors of fake news dissemination on Facebook. *Science Advances 5*(1), eaau4586.

Guess, A. M. (2021). (Almost) everything in moderation: New evidence on Americans' online media diets. *American Journal of Political Science*, 65(4), 1007–1022.

Guess, A. M., M. Lerner, B. Lyons, et al. (2020). A digital media literacy intervention increases discernment between mainstream and false news in the United States and India. *Proceeding of the National Academy of Sciences 117*(27), 15536–15545.

Guess, A. M., B. Lyons, J. M. Montgomery, B. Nyhan, and J. Reifler (2019). Fake news, Facebook ads, and misperceptions: Assessing information quality in the 2018 US midterm election campaign. https://cpb-us-e1 .wpmucdn. com/sites. dartmouth. edu/dist/5/2293/files/2021/03/fake - news- 2018.pdf.

Guess, A. M. and B. A. Lyons (2020). Misinformation, disinformation, and online propaganda. In N. Persily and J. A. Tucker (eds.), *Social Media and Democracy: The State of the Field, Prospects for Reform*, pp. 10–33. Cambridge: Cambridge University Press.

Guess, A. M., B. Nyhan, and J. Reifler (2020). Exposure to untrustworthy websites in the 2016 US election. *Nature Human Behaviour 4*(5), 472–480.

Hager, A. (2019). Do online ads influence vote choice? *Political Communication 36*(3), 376–393.

Hartmann, K. and G. Wenzelburger (2021). Uncertainty, risk and the use of algorithms in policy decisions: A case study on criminal justice in the USA. *Policy Sciences 54*(2), 269–287.

Hong, L. and S. Page (2004). Groups of diverse problem solvers can outperform groups of high-ability problem solvers. *Proceedings of the National Academy of Sciences 101*(46), 16385–16389.

Hosseinmardi, H., A. Ghasemian, A. Clauset, et al. (2020). Evaluating the scale, growth, and origins of right-wing echo chambers on YouTube. arxiv:2011.12843.

Ingrams, A. (2019). Public values in the age of big data: A public information perspective. *Policy & Internet 11*(2), 128–148.

Iyengar, S., Y. Lelkes, M. Levendusky, N. Malhotra, and S. J. Westwood (2019). The origins and consequences of affective polarization in the United States. *Annual Review of Political Science 22*(1), 129–146.

Jackson, S. J., M. Bailey, and B. Foucault Welles (2018). #GirlsLikeUs: Trans advocacy and community building online. *New Media & Society 20*(5), 1868–1888.

Jackson, S. J., M. Bailey, and B. F. Welles (2020). *#HashtagActivism: Networks of race and gender justice*. Cambridge: MIT Press.

Jackson, S. J. and B. Foucault Welles (2015). Hijacking #myNYPD: Social media dissent and networked counterpublics. *Journal of Communication 65*(6), 932–952.

Jobin, A., M. Ienca, and E. Vayena (2019). The global landscape of AI ethics guidelines. *Nature Machine Intelligence* (1), 389–399.

Jungherr, A. (2014). The logic of political coverage on Twitter: Temporal dynamics and content. *Journal of Communication 64*(2), 239–259.

Jungherr, A. (2016). Twitter use in election campaigns: A systematic literature review. *Journal of Information Technology & Politics 13*(1), 72–91.

Jungherr, A., O. Posegga, and J. An (2019). Discursive power in contemporary media systems: A comparative framework. *The International Journal of Press/Politics 59*(9), 24(4), 404–425.

Jungherr, A., G. Rivero, and D. Gayo-Avello (2020). *Retooling Politics: How Digital Media are Shaping Democracy*. New York: Cambridge University Press.

Jungherr, A. and R. Schroeder (2021). Disinformation and the structural transformations of the public arena: Addressing the actual challenges to democracy. *Social Media+ Society 7*(1), https://doi.org/10.1177/2056305121988928.

Kalla, J. L. and D. E. Broockman (2018). The minimal persuasive effects of campaign contact in general elections: Evidence from 49 field experiments. *American Political Science Review 112*(1), 148–166.

Karpf, D. (2012). Social science research methods in internet time. *Information, Communication & Society 15*(5), 639–661.

Karpf, D. (2020). How digital disinformation turned dangerous. In W. L. Bennett and S. Livingston (eds.), *The Disinformation Age: Politics, Technology, and Disruptive Communication in the United States*, pp. 153–168. New York: Cambridge University Press.

Keller, D. (2018). Internet platforms: Observations on speech, danger, and money. Hoover Working Group on National Security, Technology, and Law, Aegis Series Paper No. 1807.

King, G., J. Pan, and M. E. Roberts (2013). How censorship in China allows government criticism but silences collective expression. *American Political Science Review 107*(2), 326–343.

King, G. and N. Persily (2020). A new model for industry–academic partnerships. *PS: Political Science & Politics 53*(4), 703–709.

Kitschelt, H. and P. Rehm (2020). Political participation. In D. Caramani (ed.), *Comparative Politics* (5th ed.), pp. 318–335. Oxford: Oxford University Press.

Kleinberg, J., J. Ludwig, S. Mullainathan, and C. R. Sunstein (2020). Algorithms as discrimination detectors. *Proceedings of the National Academy of Sciences 117*(48), 30096–30100.

Klonick, K. (2020). The Facebook oversight board: Creating an independent institution to adjudicate online free expression. *Yale Law Journal 129*(8), 2418–2499.

Knill, C. and J. Tosun (2020). Policy-making. In D. Caramani (ed.), *Comparative Politics* (5th ed.), pp. 361–375. Oxford: Oxford University Press.

Krafft, T. D., K. A. Zweig, and P. D. König (2022). How to regulate algorithmic decision-making: A framework of regulatory requirements for different applications. *Regulation and Governance*, 16, 119–136.

Kreiss, D. (2021). Social media and democracy: The state of the field, prospects for reform, ed. Nathaniel Persily and Joshua A. Tucker. *The International Journal of Press/Politics*, 1–8.

Ladner, A. and J. Pianzola (2010). Do voting advice applications have an effect on electoral participation and voter turnout? Evidence from the 2007 Swiss federal elections. In *International Conference on Electronic Participation*, pp. 211–224. New York: Springer.

Langer, A. I. and J. B. Gruber (2021, June). Political agenda setting in the hybrid media system: Why legacy media still matter a great deal. *The International Journal of Press/Politics 8*, 26(2): 313–340.

Lazer, D. M., M. A. Baum, Y. Benkler, et al. (2018). The science of fake news. *Science 359*(6380), 1094–1096.

Lazer, D. M. J., A. Pentland, D. J. Watts, et al. (2020). Computational social science: Obstacles and opportunities. *Science 369*(6507), 1060–1062.

Lehdonvirta, V. and J. Bright (2015). Crowdsourcing for public policy and government. *Policy & Internet 7*(3), 263–267.

Lelkes, Y., G. Sood, and S. Iyengar (2017). The hostile audience: The effect of access to broadband internet on partisan affect. *American Journal of Political Science 61*(1), 5–20.

Levy, R. (2021). Social media, news consumption, and polarization: Evidence from a field experiment. *American Economic Review*, 111(3), 831–870.

Lewandowsky, S., M. Jetter, and U. K. Ecker (2020). Using the president's tweets to understand political diversion in the age of social media. *Nature Communications 11*(1), 1–12.

Lindgren, S. (2019). Movement mobilization in the age of hashtag activism: examining the challenge of noise, hate, and disengagement in the #MeToo campaign. *Policy & Internet 11*(4), 1–21.

Liu, H. K. (2017). Crowdsourcing government: Lessons from multiple disciplines. *Public Administration Review 77*(5), 656–667.

Liu, H. K. (2021). Crowdsourcing: Citizens as coproducers of public services. *Policy & Internet*, 13(2), 315–331.

Loomba, S., A. de Figueiredo, S. J. Piatek, K. de Graaf, and H. J. Larson (2021). Measuring the impact of COVID-19 vaccine misinformation on vaccination intent in the UK and USA. *Nature Human Behaviour 5*(3), 337–348.

Margetts, H. and P. Dunleavy (2013). The second wave of digital-era governance: A quasi-paradigm for government on the web. *Philosophical Transactions of the Royal Society A 371*(1987).

Margetts, H., P. John, S. Hale, and T. Yasseri (2016). *Political Turbulence: How Social Media Shape Collective Action*. Princeton, NJ: Princeton University Press.

Marschall, S. and D. Garzia (2014). Voting advice applications in a comparative perspective: An introduction. In D. Garzia and S. Marschall (eds.),

Matching Voters with Parties and Candidates. Voting Advice Applications in Comparative Perspective, pp. 1–10. Colchester: ECPR Press.

Matz, S. C., M. Kosinski, G. Nave, and D. J. Stillwell (2017). Psychological targeting as an effective approach to digital mass persuasion. *Proceeding of the National Academy of Sciences 114*(48), 12714–12719.

McCombs, M. E. and D. L. Shaw (1972). The agenda-setting function of mass media. *Public Opinion Quarterly 36*(2), 176–187.

McCombs, M. E. and D. L. Shaw (1993). The evolution of agenda-setting research: Twenty-five years in the marketplace of ideas. *Journal of Communication 43*(2), 58–67.

McGregor, S. C. (2019). Social media as public opinion: How journalists use social media to represent public opinion. *Journalism 20*(8), 1070–1086.

McGregor, S. C. and L. Molyneux (2020). Twitter's influence on news judgment: An experiment among journalists. *Journalism 21*(5), 597–613.

McKay, S. and C. Tenove (2020). Disinformation as a threat to deliberative democracy. *Political Research Quarterly 6*(1).

Messing, S. and S. J. Westwood (2014). Selective exposure in the age of social media. *Communication Research 41*(8), 1042–1063.

Miller, G. J. (2005). The political evolution of principal-agent models. *Annual Review of Political Science 8*, 203–225.

Molyneux, L. and S. C. McGregor (2021). Legitimating a platform: Evidence of journalists' role in transferring authority to Twitter. *Information, Communication & Society.*

Mosca, L. (2018). Democratic vision and online participatory spaces in the Italian Movimento 5 Stelle. *Acta Politica 55*(1), 1–18.

Munger, K. (2019). Knowledge decays: Temporal validity and social science in a changing world. https://osf.io/ca5wz/.

Munger, K., A. M. Guess, and E. Hargittai (2021). Quantitative description of digital media. *Journal of Quantitative Description: Digital Media 1*(1), 1–13.

Munzert, S., P. Barberá, A. M. Guess, and J. H. Yang (2021, January). Do online voter guides empower citizens? *Public Opinion Quarterly 20*(3), 227–24.

Munzert, S. and S. Ramirez-Ruiz (2021, January). Meta-analysis of the effects of voting advice applications. *Political Communication 00*(00), 1–16.

Natale, S. and A. Ballatore (2014). The web will kill them all: New media, digital utopia, and political struggle in the Italian 5-Star Movement. *Media, Culture and Society 36*(1), 105–121.

Nyhan, B. (2020). Facts and myths about misperceptions. *Journal of Economic Perspectives 34*(3), 220–236.

Nyhan, B., E. Porter, J. Reifler, and T. J. Wood (2020). Taking fact-checks literally but not seriously? The effects of journalistic fact-checking on factual beliefs and candidate favorability. *Political Behavior 42*(3), 939–960.

Nyhan, B. and J. Reifler (2010). When corrections fail: The persistence of political misperceptions. *Political Behavior 32*(2), 303–330.

Nyhan, B. and J. Reifler (2015). The effect of fact-checking on elites: A field experiment on U.S. State legislators. *American Journal of Political Science 59*(3), 628–640.

OECD (2005). e-government for better government. Technical report, OECD, Paris.

O'Neil, C. (2016). *Weapons of Math Destruction: How Big Data Increases Inequality and Threatens Democracy*. New York: Crown.

Ostfeld, M. (2017). Unity versus uniformity: Effects of targeted advertising on perceptions of group politics. *Political Communication 34*(4), 530–547.

Pan, J. and A. A. Siegel (2020). How Saudi crackdowns fail to silence online dissent. *American Political Science Review 114*(1), 109–125.

Pariser, E. (2011). *The Filter Bubble: What the Internet Is Hiding From You*. London: Penguin.

Park, S., M. Specter, N. Narula, and R. L. Rivest (2021). Going from bad to worse: From internet voting to blockchain voting. *Journal of Cybersecurity*, 7(1), tyaa025.

Pennycook, G. and D. G. Rand (2019a). Fighting misinformation on social media using crowdsourced judgments of news source quality. *Proceedings of the National Academy of Sciences of the United States of America 6*, 116(7), 2521–2526.

Pennycook, G. and D. G. Rand (2019b). Lazy, not biased: Susceptibility to partisan fake news is better explained by lack of reasoning than by motivated reasoning. *Cognition 188*, 39–50.

Persily, N. (2017). Can democracy survive the Internet? *Journal of Democracy 28*(2), 63–76.

Persily, N. (2021). Opening a window into tech: The challenge and opportunity for data transparency. Report, Stanford University.

Persily, N. and J. A. Tucker (2020a). Conclusion: The challenges and opportunities for social media research. In N. Persily and J. A. Tucker (eds.), *Social Media and Democracy: The State of the Field, Prospects for Reform*, pp. 313–331. New York: Cambridge University Press.

Persily, N. and J. A. Tucker (eds.). (2020b). *Social Media and Democracy: The State of the Field, Prospects for Reform*. New York: Cambridge University Press.

Petitpas, A., J. M. Jaquet, and P. Sciarini (2021). Does e-voting matter for turnout, and to whom? *Electoral Studies 71*, 102245.

Pianzola, J., A. H. Trechsel, K. Vassil, G. Schwerdt, and R. M. Alvarez (2019). The impact of personalized information on vote intention: Evidence from a randomized field experiment. *Journal of Politics 81*(3), 833–847.

Prpić, J., A. Taeihagh, and J. Melton (2015). The fundamentals of policy crowdsourcing. *Policy & Internet 7*(3), 340–361.

Rieder, B. and J. Hofmann (2020). Towards platform observability. *Internet Policy Review 9*(4).

Roberts, M. E. (2018). *Censored: Distraction and Diversion inside China's Great Firewall*. Princeton, NJ Princeton University Press.

Roberts, S. T. (2019, July). *Behind the Screen: Content Moderation in the Shadows of Social Media*. New Haven, CT: Yale University Press.

Rudin, C. (2019). Stop explaining black box machine learning models for high stakes decisions and use interpretable models instead. *Nature Machine Intelligence 1*(5), 206–215.

Sances, M. W. (2019). Missing the target? Using surveys to validate social media ad targeting. *Political Science Research and Methods 9*(1), 215–222.

Scharkow, M., F. Mangold, S. Stier, and J. Breuer (2020). How social network sites and other online intermediaries increase exposure to news. *Proceedings of the National Academy of Sciences of the United States of America 117*(6), 2761–2763.

Schattschneider, E. E. (1960). *The Semisovereign People: A Realist's View of Democracy in America*. New York: Holt, Rinehart and Winston.

Schaub, M. and D. Morisi (2020). Voter mobilisation in the echo chamber: Broadband internet and the rise of populism in Europe. *European Journal of Political Research 59*(4), 752–773.

Schultze, M. (2014). Effects of voting advice applications (VAAs) on political knowledge about party positions. *Policy & Internet 6*(1), 46–68.

Sears, D. O. and J. L. Freedman (1967). Selective exposure to information: A critical review. *Public Opinion Quarterly 31*(2), 194–213.

Settle, J. E. (2018). *Frenemies: How Social Media Polarizes America*. Cambridge: Cambridge University Press.

Shi, F., M. Teplitskiy, E. Duede, and J. A. Evans (2019). The wisdom of polarized crowds. *Nature Human Behaviour 3*, 329–336.

Smith, A. and P. P. Martín (2020). Going beyond the smart city? Implementing technopolitical platforms for urban democracy in Madrid and Barcelona. *Journal of Urban Technology*, 28(1–2), 311–330.

Solvak, M. and K. Vassil (2018). Could internet voting halt declining electoral turnout? New evidence that e-voting is habit forming. *Policy & Internet 10*(1), 4–21.

Stockman, C. and V. Scalia (2020). Democracy on the Five Star Movement's Rousseau platform. *European Politics and Society 21*(5), 603–617.

Sunstein, C. R. (2001). *Republic.com*. Princeton, NJ: Princeton University Press.

Sunstein, C. R. (2018). *#Republic: Divided democracy in the age of social media*. Princeton, NJ: Princeton University Press.

Taeihagh, A. (2017). Crowdsourcing: A new tool for policy-making? *Policy Sciences 50*(4), 629–647.

Taeihagh, A., M. Ramesh, and M. Howlett (2021). Assessing the regulatory challenges of emerging disruptive technologies. *Regulation and Governance*, 15(4), 1009–1019.

Ternovski, J., J. Kalla, and P. M. Aronow (2021). Deepfake warnings for political videos increase disbelief but do not improve discernment: Evidence from two experiments. https://osf.io/dta97/

Theocharis, Y. (2015). The conceptualization of digitally networked participation. *Social Media + Society*, (July-December), 1–14.

Theocharis, Y., J. Moor, and J. W. Deth (2021). Digitally networked participation and lifestyle politics as new modes of political participation. *Policy & Internet 13*(1), 30–53.

Theocharis, Y. and J. W. van Deth (2018). The continuous expansion of citizen participation: a new taxonomy. *European Political Science Review 10*(1), 139–163.

Tucker, J. A., Y. Theocharis, M. E. Roberts, and P. Barberá (2017). From liberation to turmoil: Social media and democracy. *Journal of Democracy 28*(4), 46–59.

Tufekci, Z. (2017). *Twitter and tear gas: The power and fragility of networked protest*. New Haven, CT Yale University Press.

Vaccari, C. and A. Chadwick (2020). Deepfakes and disinformation: Exploring the impact of synthetic political video on deception, uncertainty, and trust in news. *Social Media+ Society 6*(1), 1–13.

Van Deth, J. W. (2014). A conceptual map of political participation. *Acta Politica 49*(3), 349–367.

Van Duyn, E. and J. Collier (2019). Priming and fake news: The effects of elite discourse on evaluations of news media. *Mass Communication and Society 22*(1), 29–48.

Vassil, K., M. Solvak, P. Vinkel, A. H. Trechsel, and R. M. Alvarez (2016). The diffusion of internet voting: Usage patterns of internet voting in Estonia between 2005 and 2015. *Government Information Quarterly 33*(3), 453–459.

Vassil, K. and T. Weber (2011). A bottleneck model of e-voting: Why technology fails to boost turnout. *New Media & Society 13*(8), 1336–1354.

Verhulst, S. G., A. J. Zahranec, and A. Young (2019). Identifying citizens' needs by combining AI and CI. Report, The Governance Lab, New York University.

Vosoughi, S., D. Roy, and S. Aral (2018). The spread of true and false news online. *Science 359*(6380), 1146–1151.

Walgrave, S., S. Soroka, and M. Nuytemans (2008). The mass media's political agenda-setting power: A longitudinal analysis of media, parliament, and government in Belgium (1993 to 2000). *Comparative Political Studies 41*(6), 814–836.

Wardle, C. and H. Derakhshan (2017). Information disorder: Toward an interdisciplinary framework for research and policy making. Strasbourg: Council of Europe.

Watts, D. J., D. M. Rothschild, and M. Mobius (2021). Measuring the news and its impact on democracy. *Proceedings of the National Academy of Sciences 118*(15), e1912443118.

Weeks, B. E. and H. Gil de Zúñiga (2021). What's next? Six observations for the future of political misinformation research. *American Behavioral Scientist 65*(2), 277–289.

Weidmann, N. B. and E. G. Rød (2019). *The Internet and Political Protest in Autocracies*. Oxford: Oxford University Press.

Williams, B. A., C. F. Brooks, and Y. Shmargad (2018). How algorithms discriminate based on data they lack: Challenges, solutions, and policy implications. *Journal of Information Policy 8*, 78–115.

Wittenberg, C. and A. J. Berinski (2020). Misinformation and its correction. In N. Persily and J. A. Tucker (eds.), *Social Media and Democracy: The State of the Field, Prospects for Reform*, pp. 163–198. Cambridge: Cambridge University Press.

Wittenberg, C., J. Zong, D. Rand, et al. (2021). The (minimal) persuasive advantage of political video over text. Proceedings of the National Academy of Sciences, 118(47). e2114388118.

Wolfe, M., B. D. Jones, and F. R. Baumgartner (2013). A failure to communicate: Agenda setting in media and policy studies. *Political Communication 30*(2), 175–192.

Wood, T. and E. Porter (2019). The elusive backfire effect: Mass attitudes' steadfast factual adherence. *Political Behavior 41*(1), 135–163.

Woolley, A. W., C. F. Chabris, A. Pentland, N. Hashmi, and T. W. Malone (2010). Evidence for a collective intelligence factor in the performance of human groups. *Science 330*(6004), 686–688.

Woolley, S. C. and P. N. Howard (2018). *Computational Propaganda: Political Parties, Politicians, and Political Manipulation on Social Media*. Oxford: Oxford University Press.

Yang, T., S. Majó-Vázquez, R. K. Nielsen, and S. González-Bailón (2020). Exposure to news grows less fragmented with an increase in mobile access. *Proceedings of the National Academy of Sciences 117*(46), 28678–28683.

Zarsky, T. (2016). The trouble with algorithmic decisions: An analytic road map to examine efficiency and fairness in automated and opaque decision making. *Science, Technology, & Human Values 41*(1), 118–132.

Zeitzoff, T. (2017). How social media is changing conflict. *Journal of Conflict Resolution 61*(9), 1970–1991.

Zerilli, J., A. Knott, J. Maclaurin, and C. Gavaghan (2019). Transparency in algorithmic and human decision-making: Is there a double standard? *Philosophy & Technology 32*(4), 661–683.

Acknowledgments

This project received funding from the European Research Council (ERC) under the European Union's Horizon 2020 research and innovation program (grant agreement nr. 883121). I am grateful to Jonathan Klüser, Maël Kubli, Nahema Marchal, Stefan Müller, and three anonymous reviewers for helpful comments.

Cambridge Elements ☰

Public Policy

M. Ramesh
National University of Singapore (NUS)

M. Ramesh is UNESCO Chair on Social Policy Design at the Lee Kuan Yew School of Public Policy, NUS. His research focuses on governance and social policy in East and Southeast Asia, in addition to public policy institutions and processes. He has published extensively in reputed international journals. He is Co-editor of *Policy and Society* and *Policy Design and Practice*.

Michael Howlett
Simon Fraser University, British Colombia

Michael Howlett is Burnaby Mountain Professor and Canada Research Chair (Tier 1) in the Department of Political Science, Simon Fraser University. He specialises in public policy analysis, and resource and environmental policy. He is currently editor-in-chief of *Policy Sciences* and co-editor of the *Journal of Comparative Policy Analysis, Policy and Society* and *Policy Design and Practice*.

Xun WU
Hong Kong University of Science and Technology

Xun WU is Professor and Head of the Division of Public Policy at the Hong Kong University of Science and Technology. He is a policy scientist whose research interests include policy innovations, water resource management and health policy reform. He has been involved extensively in consultancy and executive education, his work involving consultations for the World Bank and UNEP.

Judith Clifton
University of Cantabria

Judith Clifton is Professor of Economics at the University of Cantabria, Spain. She has published in leading policy journals and is editor-in-chief of the *Journal of Economic Policy Reform*. Most recently, her research enquires how emerging technologies can transform public administration, a forward-looking cutting-edge project which received €3.5 million funding from the Horizon2020 programme.

Eduardo Araral
National University of Singapore (NUS)

Eduardo Araral is widely published in various journals and books and has presented in forty conferences. He is currently Co-Director of the Institute of Water Policy at the Lee Kuan Yew School of Public Policy, NUS, and is a member of the editorial board of *Journal of Public Administration Research and Theory* and the board of the Public Management Research Association.

About the Series

Elements in Public Policy is a concise and authoritative collection of assessments of the state of the art and future research directions in public policy research, as well as substantive new research on key topics. Edited by leading scholars in the field, the series is an ideal medium for reflecting on and advancing the understanding of critical issues in the public sphere. Collectively, the series provides a forum for broad and diverse coverage of all major topics in the field while integrating different disciplinary and methodological approaches.

Cambridge Elements ≡

Public Policy

Elements in the Series

Printed in the United States
by Baker & Taylor Publisher Services